OUR
GREAT
PURPOSE

OUR GREAT PURPOSE

*

ADAM SMITH
on LIVING
A BETTER LIFE

Ryan Patrick Hanley

PRINCETON UNIVERSITY PRESS
PRINCETON AND OXFORD

Published by Princeton University Press
41 William Street, Princeton, New Jersey 08540
6 Oxford Street, Woodstock, Oxfordshire OX20 1TR

press.princeton.edu

Library of Congress Cataloging-in-Publication Data
Names: Hanley, Ryan Patrick, 1974– author.
Title: Our great purpose : Adam Smith on living a better life /
Ryan Patrick Hanley.
Description: Princeton : Princeton University Press, [2019] |
Includes bibliographical references and index.
Identifiers: LCCN 2019018023 | ISBN 9780691179445
(hardcover : acid-free paper)
Subjects: LCSH: Smith, Adam, 1723–1790. | Conduct of life. | Life.
Classification: LCC B1545.Z7 H365 2019 | DDC 170/.44—dc23
LC record available at https://lccn.loc.gov/2019018023

ISBN (e-book) 978-0-691-19775-3

British Library Cataloging-in-Publication Data is available

Jacket Image: Adam Smith, engraving, 1970. Courtesy of the
Library of Congress

This book has been composed in Garamond Premier Pro

Printed on acid-free paper ∞

Printed in the United States of America

1 3 5 7 9 10 8 6 4 2

For my daughter

Contents

——— ✶ ———

OUR
GREAT
PURPOSE

Introduction

✳

What does it mean to "live a better life"? And for that matter, what exactly does it mean to "live a life" in the first place? These are hardly easy questions to answer. And they certainly aren't easy things to do. But at the very least, it seems to me, living a life requires that we be actively engaged in pursuing a trajectory that we can recognize as "a life"—that is, a trajectory that not only has a beginning and middle and end, but also has a unity to it that enables us to see all its different parts as fitting together in a meaningful way.

Some people are better at this than others. But a lot hangs on whether we can do it well. Each of us, after all, has been given only one life to live. So as we each live this single life that is ours, we have to make all sorts of choices about what paths to follow and not follow. But what makes one path better than another? What standard should we use to judge what choices to make? And where should we turn for guidance on all of this?

This book suggests we can find an excellent guide to these questions in Adam Smith. This is likely to strike many people as surprising. Adam Smith of course is famous today as a founding father of capitalism, not for his ideas on how to live a life. But as I show below, Smith in fact has much to offer us on this front. In particular, Smith's philosophy of living (and I do think we're right to speak of his thought in this way) is founded on a synthesis of action and reflection—or, to use Smith's own words, a synthesis of "wisdom" and "virtue."[1]

Smith's belief that living a good life requires bringing together action and reflection not only is central to his philosophy of living, but also distinguishes his project from other sorts of efforts in this vein. Modern readers, when they hear talk of living good lives, may expect a self-help book, the sort of thing that outlines (in the words of one recently popular exemplar) a set of "rules for life."[2] But Smith never sought to write a self-help book, even if some of his readers have tried to read him this way. Smith's first biographer once said of his main work in moral philosophy that "with the theoretical doctrines of the book, there are everywhere interwoven, with singular taste and address, the purest and most elevated maxims concerning the practical conduct of life."[3] A century later, no less a figure than the future U.S. president Woodrow Wilson would reiterate the same lesson in some of his university lectures at Princeton, claiming that Smith "stores his volumes full with the sagest practical maxims, fit to have fallen from the lips of the shrewdest of those Glasgow merchants in whose society he learned so much."[4] But for all this we do Smith an injustice if we reduce his concerns with the philosophy of living to practical maxims of the sort one finds in the work of Smith's friend Benjamin Franklin or in today's self-help books. Smith, to put it bluntly, knew that there is all the difference in the world between learning how to get ahead in life and learning how to live life well.

Smith's books then have something to offer to the busy and upwardly mobile.[5] But they have more to offer, I think, to a different sort of reader, after something different than easy advice, quick fixes, and lists of rules. This book presents Smith's wisdom on this front to the sort of readers who will welcome not only an opportunity to see Smith in a new way, but also an opportunity to see how seeing Smith in this new way might lead them to see themselves and their own lives in a new way.

And that we will be seeing Smith in a new way is clear. Smith's philosophy of living has not been a prominent element of the voluminous scholarship on his thought. Some of the very best scholars of his thought in fact have argued that Smith thinks the aim of moral philosophy is merely to provide "an account of the origin and function" of our moral concepts, and as a result, "if we want guidance on how to live the good life, we should look elsewhere."[6] It will be obvious from what follows that I have a different view. But my goal in this book isn't to settle scholarly scores. I've contributed to the scholarly debates in my other books and articles on Smith, which include all the citations and detailed footnotes to the specialized literature that contributions to such debates require. But my goal here is different.[7] In presenting Smith as a wise guide to living a life, I cast some light on some sides of his thought that have received relatively less attention, and I hope this may be of interest to specialists. But more importantly, I hope that by presenting Smith in this way, readers of this book will have an opportunity to spend some time with—indeed live with—a thinker who has a great deal to show us about our own lives and what we do well to think about if we hope to live them as well as we can. I first encountered Adam Smith a quarter century ago, and I know my own life is better for the years I've lived with him. I hope this might in time prove true for you as well.

* * *

This book is of course about Smith's thoughts on living a life. As such, it does not aspire to provide a full treatment of Smith's own life or his thought. But insofar as the story of his life and the broader themes of his thought are not irrelevant to our focus, a very brief introduction to his life and his ideas may be useful.[8]

Smith was born in 1723 in the coastal town of Kirkcaldy, just north of Edinburgh. His father died before he was born, leaving him to be raised by his devoted and loving mother. After receiving an excellent early education at his local parish school, he was sent to study at the University of Glasgow. Here he completed his undergraduate studies, in part under the tutelage of his beloved teacher Francis Hutcheson, widely regarded today as the father of what has come to be known as the Scottish Enlightenment. After finishing at Glasgow in 1740, Smith received a scholarship to Oxford to continue his studies in preparation for a career as a minister. But Oxford disappointed him, and he returned to Scotland in 1746.

Back in Scotland, instead of pursuing a career in the church, Smith delivered a series of public lectures on rhetoric. These earned him sufficient attention to be considered for a professorship at Glasgow, a position that he was awarded and began in 1751. At Glasgow Smith lectured on subjects ranging from rhetoric and belles lettres to natural theology and logic and jurisprudence. But it was chiefly as a teacher of moral philosophy that he came to be known. Smith's career at Glasgow as both an admired teacher and an able administrator continued until 1764, when he resigned his university post in order to take up a position as traveling tutor to the Duke of Buccleuch. In the company of the duke, Smith spent the next two years in France as the duke's guide on his Grand Tour. It would be his only trip outside Great Britain, but for the francophile Smith it was momentous, especially as it enabled him to meet and talk with many of the leading figures of the Enlightenment.

While in France, Smith started writing a book. This continued to occupy him for the decade after his return to Scotland in 1766. And after its completion and publication, Smith went on to hold a civil post in Edinburgh, serving the Crown as a collector of customs, a post he held until his death. In these final Edinburgh years, Smith lived a happy life as a man of letters, meeting with his friends and hosting visitors in the home he shared with his mother and cousin. This residence, Panmure House, still stands in Edinburgh, and it was here that Smith would end his days in 1790, shortly after sending to press his final revisions of his first book.

Smith led a quiet life. We do have a few funny anecdotes about him—including one about the time he fell into a tanning pit while expostulating on the benefits of specialized labor, another about the time he was lost in thought and tried to make tea out of bread, and another about the time he went wandering about in the countryside, oblivious to the fact that he was still in his nightclothes. These have fostered an image of Smith as the classic absent-minded professor. And in truth, unwed and childless, modest and retiring, Smith's life really was one of books and ideas. We get a sense of this from the engraving on the stone marking his burial place in Edinburgh's Canongate churchyard, steps from Panmure House. In its entirety it reads, "Here are deposited the remains of Adam Smith, author of *The Theory of Moral Sentiments* and *Wealth of Nations*: He was born, 5th June, 1723. And he died 17th July, 1790." The inscription captures the essential truth of Smith's life: namely that it lies mainly in his two published books, which together compose the essentials of his system.

Smith's second book, the *Wealth of Nations*—the one begun in France and published in 1776—is the one for which he is known today. Smith intended it first and foremost as an intervention in the most prominent debate in political economy of his day, the debate over free trade, and specifically the system of trade protectionism known as mercantilism. The *Wealth of Nations* is adamantly hostile to mercantilism, arguing it serves merely to line the pockets of wealthy and well-connected special interests, at a direct cost to the interests of less elite and less well-to-do consumers. Yet the *Wealth of Nations* was hardly just a tract for its times. Smith's critique of protectionism was founded on his belief in the efficiency of the "system of natural liberty," and indeed it is as a defense of this system that the book has left its lasting mark. As a result, Adam Smith's name has been, for generations of students of economics, synonymous with the defense of such doctrines as the superior productivity of specialized labor, the mutual gains between buyers and sellers (and indeed nations) that free exchange makes possible, and the dangers of excessive government intervention in market processes.

Yet even though Smith owes his fame to the *Wealth of Nations*, it is his other book that is our focus in what follows. In 1759, Smith published the first edition of *The Theory of Moral Sentiments*. The book had its origin in Smith's lectures to the students in his moral philosophy class at Glasgow. Some trace of this is evident in the text, which concludes with a long chapter on the history of various moral theories: an approach to the history of ideas common enough today though novel for its time. Yet the real significance and originality of the book lies elsewhere. In particular, in *The Theory of Moral Sentiments*, Smith developed an original theory of moral judgment, the cornerstone of which is his concept of sympathy: the sentiment that leads us to feel, in some measure and to some degree, what other people feel, and which Smith thinks is inherent to human nature. Sympathy, in turn, is assisted by another mechanism: the figure Smith called the "impartial spectator," an ideal judge whose judgment is unclouded by distorting feelings, and thus deliberates calmly and coolly about right and wrong. But as we will see, alongside this theory of moral judgment, *The Theory of Moral Sentiments* also lays out a philosophy of living founded on a particular understanding of what it means to have a virtuous character—a philosophy of living that is much indebted to ancient reflections on virtue going back to Plato and Aristotle and the Stoics, but which is very consciously tailored for our modern world.

* * *

To present Smith's philosophy of living as effectively as possible, what follows is organized into a series of short chapters. Each focuses on a single line from one of Smith's writings (most often *The Theory of Moral Sentiments*) and after presenting this line I offer a short commentary on it. In so doing I hope, among other things, to allow Smith's genius as a writer to shine through. A student of classical rhetoric and a lover of modern literature, Smith wrote beautiful prose. And while he didn't set out to write aphorisms, his sentences are often subtle and sophisticated, and in many cases merit sustained reflection. In any case, by presenting his thought in this way, I offer an accessible point of entry to those encountering his writings for the first time, as well as a new lens through which veterans might reencounter his texts and thought. Also, each of these quotations stands on its own, and can be read independently of the others. But both my presentation of them and my commentaries on them have been arranged and ordered in such a way as to tell a story that starts with the first chapter and ends with the last.

In selecting these quotations I have been guided by my sense of what Smith took to be the key challenges to living a life today. Speaking broadly, these challenges fall into two groups. First are those that come from the way we as human beings have been made. On this front, Smith frequently returns to the idea that we are by nature often led in two very different directions. On the one hand, we are naturally led to be concerned with ourselves and our own well-being. On the other hand, we are naturally led to be concerned with the well-being and happiness of others. A second set of challenges comes from the world that we live in today. Like the challenges that come from our nature, these challenges involve competing demands that pull us in different ways. As we all likely know very well, our world rewards efforts to get ahead, bestowing upon the successful wealth, status, and power. Yet even today we value behavior that sacrifices self-interest, especially when this advances the well-being of others. All of this is to say that both our natures and the nature of our world pull us in different directions, all at once. These competing demands raise key challenges to the project of living a single and unified life, and thus one of the recurring themes in what follows is division and unity.

But diagnosing the challenges to living well is only half of Smith's insight into living a life. Thus in selecting these quotations I have also been guided by my sense of what Smith thought we need to do, in our lives, if we hope to overcome these challenges. First, in his view, we need to adopt certain virtues. Some of these are virtues that have to do with our feelings toward ourselves; the virtues of prudence and self-command play important roles in this process. Others have to do with our feelings and actions toward others, with justice and benevolence playing especially important roles here. Another set of recurring themes in what follows then are the two sets of virtues that enable us to live a good and unified life: what Smith calls the "awful virtues" of magnanimity and self-command, and the "amiable virtues" of benevolence and love.

At the same time, living a life, Smith teaches, requires more than adopting certain virtues—as tough a task as that is. For in order to adopt these virtues, we need to be able to see ourselves anew, Smith thinks. In particular, we need to develop a critical distance from ourselves. By so doing, not only do we come to see ourselves in a new and impartial light, but we also learn how to see ourselves as others see us. It is no exaggeration to say that Smith thinks that liberal commercial society depends on the ability of its citizens to do this. But the claim I make here is both more modest and more ambitious. For Smith, living a life requires the capacity to see and reflect on our lives. Living a life requires then more than just the activity of living. It also requires us to step outside ourselves from time to time so that we can see ourselves in that impartial light in which the rest of the world sees us. This is important, as scholars have long realized, if we hope to tamp down some of our selfishness. But this act of critical reflection is also what enables us to see ourselves as a self, engaged in the project of living a life of virtue and flourishing, of unity and coherence, and thus, hopefully, of purpose and meaning.

I

———— ✳ ————

"Every man is, no doubt, by nature, first and principally
recommended to his own care; and as he is fitter to take care of
himself than of any other person, it is fit and right that it should be so."

Or: self-interest is part of human nature,
but it's a self-interest of a very particular sort.

Self-interest drives capitalism. Capitalism's friends and foes
agree on this, even if they agree on nothing else. Ask a defender
of capitalism why capitalism is preferable to socialism. You'll
be told that it's because human beings are naturally self-
interested, and that we should live in a system that rewards
what is natural to us. Ask one of capitalism's critics why we
should prefer socialism. You'll be told it's because capitalism
rewards our lowest and most selfish impulses and crowds out
higher goods such as justice and equality. Both sides thus seem
to agree that the guiding tenet of capitalism is that "greed is
good," as Michael Douglas's character Gordon Gekko memorably proclaimed in the movie *Wall Street*.

But what exactly is "self-interest"? Adam Smith has some
useful light to shed on the question. Smith himself is often regarded as a champion of self-interest; the Nobel laureate
George Stigler once wrote that self-interest is the "granite"
upon which Smith's entire system is built.[1] But we have to be

careful here. Smith does think self-interest is natural to us. This is clear enough from the quote above, in which he tells us that "every man" is "by nature" first and foremost concerned with "his own care." In some deep sense then, it's right to say that he thinks we're "hardwired" to be self-interested. But it's also pretty clear that what Smith means by this is very different from what Dr. Stigler and Mr. Gekko are after.

First, look at what Smith thinks self-interest naturally leads us to pursue. The goal of someone driven by natural self-interest, Smith says, is "his own care." We might make the same point today by saying that such a person is "taking care of herself." By this we usually mean that such a person takes good care of her health: she eats well, doesn't drink too much, gets sufficient exercise and sleep, and so on. But that's exactly what Smith thinks we're all led by nature first and foremost to do: to attend to our basic needs, and especially the needs of our bodies that we have to satisfy in order to stay alive. He says as much later: "the preservation and healthful state of the body seem to be the objects which Nature first recommends to the care of every individual."[2]

The key point here is that our needs are different from our wants. Our body's needs have been determined by nature, and are limited to specific goods: nourishment, rest, and so forth. Our wants and desires, however, come from somewhere else. Very few people, I suspect, even if they think it's reasonable to want a Ferrari rather than a Ford, would say that it's "natural" to want a Ferrari. In any case, and what matters for us, is that Smith's claim here isn't that it's natural to want a Ferrari. The self-interest he thinks natural to us is the self-interest that prompts self-care, rather than the self-interest that Mr. Gekko calls "greed."

Second, in claiming that self-interest is natural, Smith doesn't quite come out and say that self-interest is good. Again, going back to Mr. Gekko: his claim isn't just that greed is natural, but that greed is "good." Those who say this could mean to say at least two different things. They might mean that greed is *useful* to society, perhaps insofar as greed-driven consumer behavior stimulates higher productivity and creates a wealthier society. But they might mean that greed is somehow *moral* or *ethical*, and that what we often call a vice is really a virtue—as suggested by the title of Ayn Rand's book *The Virtue of Selfishness*. Which (if either) position is Smith's?

There's a fair amount of evidence that suggests Smith agrees with the first claim. In *The Theory of Moral Sentiments* (to say nothing of the *Wealth of Nations*) he tells us that "it is well that nature" has made us self-interested, as it "rouses and keeps in continual motion the industry of mankind." And this industry, in turn, has real benefits to society as a whole. Specifically, the rich, despite (or maybe because of) "their natural selfishness and rapacity," in time "divide with the poor" the wealth that their self-interested activity has created. The famous invisible hand enters at this point, with Smith explaining that the rich "are led by an invisible hand to make nearly the same distribution of the necessaries of life, which would have been made, had the earth been divided into equal portions among all its inhabitants." In short, the self-interest of some provides all with the "necessaries of life." Self-interest thus not only advances the individual's interests, but also advances "the interest of the society."[3]

So Smith clearly thinks self-interest is useful. But does he think it's also good in a moral sense? Here we need to be careful. The short answer is that it depends. It depends in particular on how we go about pursuing our self-interest. Smith later will explicitly say that "regard to our own private happiness and interest" can seem "upon many occasions very laudable principles of action," and that certain actions driven by "self-interested motives" in fact "deserve the esteem and appro-bation of every body."[4] But Smith was hardly naïve. He knew quite well that people driven by the hope of attaining "those great objects of self-interest" are often led to act in ways that are "not only unjust but extravagant."[5] So at the very least Smith's position on the goodness of self-interest is more nu-anced than Mr. Gekko's. Self-interest, he thinks, can be pur-sued in a moral way. But it can also be (and often is) pursued in an immoral way. A key part of the challenge of living life well consists in understanding the difference between these two ways—a point to which we will return in what follows.

One last point about self-interest deserves mention here. Smith's quote ends with the claim that every person is "fitter and abler to take care of himself than of any other person."[6] This can be taken in two senses. First, it could be seen as say-ing that we can each take care of ourselves more effectively than anybody else can take care of us. It could also be read as saying we can each take care of ourselves more effectively than we can take care of other people. Smith himself, I think, agrees with both points. The key idea, here and elsewhere, involves personal responsibility—the notion that we are each our own best caretakers, and that everything goes better when we ap-preciate that other people are the best caretakers of their own selves as well. This is another point to which we'll have reason to return. But for now, the main point is that Smith indeed thinks we are naturally self-interested. Yet what he means by this is something very specific, and indeed something much more limited than what we're often talking about when we talk about self-interest and capitalism today.

II

***

"How selfish soever man may be supposed, there are evidently some principles in his nature, which interest him in the fortune of others, and render their happiness necessary to him."

Or: by nature we are not only self-interested;
we're also naturally interested in others.

Self-interest, Adam Smith thinks, is natural to us—as we've seen. But it's hardly the only thing that is natural to us. For in addition to caring about our own well-being, we also naturally care about the well-being of others. As Smith says in the quote above, there seem to be "some principles" in our nature that lead us to care about others, and lead us to take an "interest" in their fortunes. Now, just what these principles are is something that Smith will of course have to explain. He should probably also say something about how he came to think this; for now he just tells us it's self-evident. But none of this should lead us to lose sight of his main point here, a point that is simple but crucial: namely that self-interest is only part of our nature. The other part of our nature is our interest in others.

This is a striking and important claim. It's striking and important partly because it's being made by Adam Smith of all people. Given his popular reputation, no one is surprised when he talks about how we're naturally self-interested, as he did in the quote that was the focus of the previous chapter. But the quote for this chapter may come as a bit of a shock to those accustomed to seeing Smith as the patron saint of self-interest. Yet clearly it is Smith saying this, and it's hardly a throw-away line, something easily dismissed as outside of his real concerns. In fact, this line is the very first line of *The Theory of Moral Sentiments*, which suggests how important it is to him. You could put it this way. We tend to be introduced to Smith today via his popular reputation as a champion of self-interest. Smith himself, on the other hand, introduces his book on ethics by calling attention to our interest in others. The lens through which Smith wants us to see moral life is that of our natural interest in others, rather than our self-interest alone.

Smith's claim is also striking for a second reason. So far we've described what Smith is talking about here as an "interest in others" or "concern for others." That seems fair given the language he uses here. At the same time, these terms fall short of capturing all of what he's after. This is partly because talk of "interest" is dispassionate. To say that we have not only self-interest but also an "interest" in others is to speak the language of contemporary social science and its clinical discussions of "egoism" and "altruism." Now, social scientific study of egoism and altruism has given rise to many important insights, and I hardly want to minimize its import. Yet it's important to see that Smith is making a stronger claim here than what most social scientists today wish to make.[1] Smith's key point here—his radical point—isn't simply that we have a natural altruistic interest in others. It's much stronger than that. What nature has in fact given us is an interest in others that is so strong and so powerful that "their happiness" is "necessary" to us.

This is a powerful claim for several reasons. First and foremost, when Smith says that others' happiness is "necessary" to us, he goes a long way toward breaking down the distinctions that we tend to make between individual and community, self and society. We today tend to assume that self and society are distinct. But Smith pushes back against this. In some deep sense, all of us, even in seeking to realize our individuality, are bound to the people around us in inescapable ways. This has important social and political implications, of course. If the happiness of others in our communities is really "necessary" to us, then a lot of familiar policies—and especially those that privilege the well-being of one group or class at the expense of others—will need to be rethought. But for now what matters is that Smith entirely rejects the idea that there's some sort of zero-sum relationship between my happiness and yours. It's simply not the case that I can be fully happy when I know that you are really miserable. And this he thinks is true of even the most self-centered people in our world. "How selfish soever" they might be, even they are happier when the people they live with are happier.

But for all this, there is another reason why Smith's claim here is so important. And this concerns its implications for the main question that is our focus in this book. Our focus again is the challenge of living a life—a life conceived as a unity, one we can see as bringing together and synthesizing all of our different parts.[2] That sounds well and good. But in this opening line of *The Theory of Moral Sentiments* Smith gives us a hint as to just how hard this is going to be. This is because we have, by nature, two parts to us that on their face pull in different directions. One leads us to care about ourselves and our own happiness, while the other leads us to care about others and their happiness. Later in the book Smith will come back to this, telling us that "the great division of our affections is into the selfish and the benevolent."[3] That's a simple observation. But this "great division" may in fact be one of the biggest challenges that our efforts to live a unified life must face.

After all, if we weren't divided in this way, life would be easy. If we only cared about our own selves, we'd always know what to do. Without any other conflicting feelings to get in the way, we could take one self-interested path through life and forget about everyone else. That might not be a good life, but it's at least a consistent life. So too, if we only cared about the happiness and well-being of others and never gave any thought to ourselves, we could dedicate ourselves wholeheartedly to the well-being and happiness of others. Then our self-interest would never get in the way of our devotion to our fellow human beings. But the truth is that neither of these paths is open to us if we genuinely hope to do justice to both sides of our nature. Unless we're ready to sacrifice half of what nature has made each of us to be—and I suspect most of us aren't—we're going to have to find a way to live that allows us to realize both sides of our nature, our concern for ourselves and our concern for others.

much unless they're followed by the hard work it takes to realize the objects of our wishes. It's too easy for that kind of person to feel good about himself just because he feels bad for others. But Smith thinks there's nothing to admire in that. What really deserve our praise and admiration are not the warm feelings we can feel in private or in a passive state, but the "action" and "exertion" that take effort and energy. And Smith leaves no doubt that the work will be hard, telling us in the line that follows that someone who wants to live up to this will have to "call forth the whole vigor of his soul" and "strain every nerve." Living this sort of life will not be for the faint of heart.

Now, there's a lot that could be said about Smith's distinction between feeling and acting here. A philosopher with some Latin might describe the difference that Smith is describing as one between benevolence and beneficence. But for us, what most matters in this distinction between mere good willing and actual good doing is how it leads Smith to make a much stronger claim about human nature than what we have seen so far from him. In the previous chapter, we saw him claim that we have a natural "interest" in the fortunes of others. But here he suggests that nature has given us something considerably stronger than a dispassionate "interest" in others' well-being. Our interest in others is something more than a mere warm feeling. It's even something more than a high-minded, idealistic altruism. These dispositions are passive. Smith, in contrast, thinks our natural concern for others is active—the sort of thing that motivates us and shapes what we do, and ultimately how we live.

Another key element of this claim concerns the goal of this action. Its goal, Smith tells us, is to promote "changes in the external circumstances of both himself and others." Smith doesn't quite spell out all of what he means here when he talks

III

———— ✳ ————

"Man was made for action, and to promote by the exertion of his faculties such changes in the external circumstances of both himself and others, as may seem most favourable to the happiness of all."

Or: we are made not merely to be interested in others, but to act for others.

This has always struck me as one of the most surprising and important lines in all of Adam Smith's writings. It makes a very bold claim, one that you'd never expect if you knew Smith only as the champion of some sort of caricatured capitalism built on selfishness. His assertion, put simply, concerns human nature. Specifically it's that we've been made to act for others, as well as for ourselves. Clearly this is something that our friend Gordon Gekko could never get on board with. But to see just how far it goes beyond his views, we need to break it down into its several parts.

First, Smith's point here rests on a specific and explicit distinction. This concerns the difference between feeling for others and acting for others. Smith, as it turns out, has little good to say about the kind of person who merely feels for others—the kind who likes to profess (and often very loudly professes) his "good inclinations and kind wishes," and is prone to "fancy himself the friend of mankind, because in his heart he wishes well." For Smith, good wishes don't count for very about these changes in external circumstances. But he does give us a few clues. First, in referencing "external circumstances," he suggests that the focus of our action for others is their practical welfare. That is, when we act for them, we're not trying to get inside their heads. We're not trying to change their ideas or get them to adopt different values or to see the light. Instead we're trying to do what we can to bring some relief to their current condition—perhaps by doing what we can to relieve the sorts of pains that poverty or illness or sadness can bring. Further, the people to whom we're trying to bring relief aren't far-distant others, but those around us—that is, our neighbors, the people we live with, and whose lives can be most directly helped (and indeed harmed) by our direct action.

In any case, our mandate is to ensure that whatever we do, we act in a way that we promote those changes that are "most favourable to the happiness of all." This is important. The claim here is that as we act, we need to make sure that our actions don't promote the well-being of any one specific group or any one specific individual (including ourselves) at the expense of the well-being of other groups or other individuals (including ourselves). This becomes especially clear in Smith's explicit reminder that the human being is made to promote the external circumstances of "both himself and others." Put differently, we're not made simply to sacrifice ourselves for others, nor are we made to sacrifice others' interests to our own. Neither perfect altruism nor perfect egoism is suited to us (or even possible for us) given the way we've been made. What we're called to do instead is to act in a way that does justice to the legitimate claims of both our own selves and those of others. Again, finding the right balance between these potentially competing interests lies at the heart of the project of living life well.

Third and finally, Smith here makes a remarkable point about the way we've been made. I introduced this above by saying that Smith is making a point about human nature. But that doesn't capture the full force of what he's after. It's easy enough to say that we have certain inborn dispositions in us, passions and instincts that are part of our "nature." But Smith is making an even stronger point here. It's that we have in fact been "made for" something. Of all that could be said about this, at the very least we can say that Smith thinks we are creatures who have been made for a purpose, and that purpose isn't just gratifying our personal needs and wants.

IV

---- ✳ ----

"Of such mighty importance does it appear to be, in the imaginations of men, to stand in that situation which sets them most in the view of general sympathy and attention."

Or: our bodily needs hardly exhaust our wants, and most of all we want attention.

We are naturally both self-interested and interested in others—that much we know already. But what exactly is it that self-interested people want? In the first chapter we saw that, above all else, naturally self-interested beings like ourselves aim to satisfy their bodily needs. But clearly we have wants that go well beyond these needs. And one of these wants—perhaps the most important of these wants—is the desire that Smith describes here, our desire for "sympathy and attention."

So what then are "sympathy" and "attention"? Sympathy turns out to be one of the most important concepts in *The Theory of Moral Sentiments*. But for Smith sympathy has a precise and somewhat unique meaning, and would require a study of its own if we hope to do full justice to it. For our purposes here, suffice it to say that Smith regards sympathy as an innate disposition, one with which we're all born, and which leads us to desire and seek out what Smith likes to call "fellow-feeling" with others. And this desire for sympathy leads us, Smith thinks, always to try to "place ourselves in the situation of another man, and view it, as it were, with his eyes and from his station."[1] This makes sympathy fundamental to Smith's social and political vision. It also suggests a way in which this social and political vision might be worth our engagement today, living as we do in an age in which we seem ever less inclined, in our cultural and political debates, to make the effort to try to see the world from the perspective of and through the eyes of those with whom we disagree.

But as important as this is, I want to leave this side of sympathy aside here and focus instead on another side of sympathy, one that is more central to our main focus on living a life. For Smith, sympathy is also a good, something that we are naturally concerned to get from others. That is, not only are we naturally disposed to sympathize with others, we also naturally desire that others sympathize with us. And this side of sympathy is captured well by the other concept that Smith pairs it with here: "attention." Now, when Smith uses the word "attention," he has something in mind that's not dissimilar from what contemporary philosophers have in mind when they speak of "recognition." But I'd like to stick with the word "attention," both because it's the word that Smith himself uses and because attention is a concept more or less familiar to all of us. What Smith describes here is the simple fact that we want other people to "pay attention" to us, to look at us and see us. We like feeling their eyes on us, and for that reason we are eager to occupy the space that allows us, as Smith says, to be "most in the view" of others.

Smith seems to me to get something profoundly right about us and our world here. People like being the center of attention, now more than ever. Yes, of course, citizens of the ancient Greek polis and of ancient Rome competed for attention. The struggle for glory and for recognition and for superiority was fundamental to ancient honor cultures, and extends all the way up to the obsession with grandeur and splendor that defined the royal courts of early modern Europe that so fascinated Smith.[2] But something changed in Smith's time, and that change has come to define our world today. In part it's that glory and honor used to be the province of the elite. But the attention that Smith describes is a very democratic phenomenon, the sort of thing that everyone wants. And, to some degree, it's also the sort of thing that everyone today can have. The whole phenomenon of social media—arguably the defining phenomenon of our age—is driven by this desire for attention. My better self would like to think that the purpose of social media is to promote human connectivity and to share meaningful content. But in the end I suspect that it is the lure of followers and "likes" that drives most posters to post: the quantifiable measures of that very "attention" that Smith knew is of such "mighty importance" to us.

All of this raises a few questions. First, what exactly should we make of this desire for attention? Is it a good thing or a bad thing? Smith doesn't come right out and make any judgment of this sort. At this point, he's not really interested in celebrating it or castigating it, in playing up its good effects or in lamenting its bad effects. He'll do that later, to be sure. Here he simply notes the phenomenon. Good empiricist that he is, his studies have led him to see something, to be struck by how important this desire for attention "appears to be" to so many people.

A second question concerns where this interest in attention comes from. Smith says something interesting here on this front. He doesn't here say, as he did with regard to our interest in preserving our bodily health, that this interest in attention has been given to us by "nature." Instead he says that our interest in the attention of others comes to us from our "imaginations." This needs some thinking through. What does it mean to say that our imagination leads us to want something? At the very least, Smith is signaling here that our desire for attention comes from a very different place than our desires for health and self-preservation. Where our desires for those basic goods were prompted by the needs of our bodies, our desire for this new good has its roots in our imagination.

This has an important implication. Our bodily desires have certain limits. To stay alive, we need a certain amount of nourishment. But after a certain point, we don't gain anything—and even worse, we're harmed—if we have too much nourishment. The body has its limits. The imagination, on the other hand, is essentially limitless. Among its other unique features, imagination can transcend physical limits, and can move about, as it were, without regard to the limits of time and space. This enables it to do certain things that no other part of our selves can do. But its limitlessness also means that there may be no limits to what it wants. So while it's easy enough to determine how much nourishment we need to stay healthy, it's not easy at all to determine how much attention we'll need to be happy. Calories can be counted just like Twitter followers. But with the former we can say when enough is enough. But it's not quite so easy to say—with apologies to Tolstoy—how many Twitter followers a man needs.

One last point about the imagination. In our language, we describe things that come from the imagination as "imaginary." Our desire for attention comes from the imagination. So does this mean that attention is something "imaginary"? We'd be wrong to dismiss it too fast like this. But putting the question this way compels us to ask ourselves several other questions that we need to answer as we make our way living our lives, namely: Do we in fact need the attention of others to live well? Is this attention of others that we are led by our imaginations to want really necessary to us in the same way that health is necessary to us? Or is it maybe something that we can do without altogether? Or might there even be some sort of middle ground here? Are some types of attention better, and even better for us, than others? All of these questions need answering before we can really know how far we should go in pursuing our self-interest.

V

---- ✳ ----

"What are the advantages which we propose by that great
purpose of human life which we call bettering our condition?
To be observed, to be attended to, to be taken notice of with
sympathy, complacency, and approbation, are all the advantages
which we can propose to derive from it."

*Or: to get the attention that we imagine we want,
we strive to make money and rise in status.*

Our bodies need physical goods, but our imaginations want
more. They lead us to crave attention. But how do we get this
attention? What sorts of things do we need to do if we want
other people to pay attention to us? Here Smith tells us. In
order "to be observed" and "to be attended to" we go about
"bettering our condition."

So what does it mean to "better our condition"? In his main
book on the subject, the *Wealth of Nations*, Smith explains
that "an augmentation of fortune is the means by which the
greater part of men propose and wish to better their condition."[1] The point is simple enough: most people who seek attention will try to get it by making money. They assume that
the kind of "condition" that matters is social status—as op-
posed to, say, the condition of our bodies or minds or souls.
And they assume that the best way to improve condition of

this sort is by making money and getting rich. In fact, there might not be much else to the ambition to get rich than this desire for attention and increased status, according to Smith. "The rich man glories in his riches," he tells us, "because he feels that they naturally draw upon him the attention of the world."[2]

Now this is a big claim. We can probably all imagine several reasons why people might want to be rich. Maybe they like the expensive things money can buy. Maybe they want to provide their families with the security that wealth brings. Maybe they want the leisure that early retirement affords. But Smith doesn't say these things, at least here. His claim is that we want to be rich so that others will pay attention to us—that "it is chiefly from this regard to the sentiments of mankind, that we pursue riches and avoid poverty."[3]

This is a central idea of Smith's, one to which he'll return when he reminds us that the "sole advantage" of wealth and greatness is that they gratify our "love of distinction."[4] But why does he think this is so important? Perhaps for two very different but maybe not incompatible reasons. On the one hand, there is something that is very encouraging about all of this. Smith has told us that we want attention. He's then told us that the best way to get this attention is through pursuing wealth. If that's right, it wouldn't be unreasonable for us to think ourselves very lucky to live in a commercial world that affords us abundant opportunities to do what we need to do in order to get what we want.

This side of the claim is all the more meaningful when we realize that it's not just the richest of the rich—the notorious one percent—who benefit from living in such a world. In fact, a world that brings people out of poverty and into even very moderate levels of opulence is a world that brings the gratification of recognition to many more than just the elite. Though you might not know it from his popular reputation, Smith was deeply troubled by the plight of the poor. In fact much of his defense of market society rests on the benefits he thinks it can bring to the poor. And part of what troubled Smith about poverty is how the poor are treated, a treatment he describes vividly in the section from which this chapter's quote is drawn. Here he explains that poverty places a poor man "out of the sight of mankind"—he is "overlooked" and forced to "live in obscurity," as the better-off "turn their eyes away from him."

Smith here nicely captures a very common phenomenon: that the wealthy are often worshipped, and the poor willfully overlooked. And when we put it this way, it's clear that there's a lot at stake in this connection of wealth and attention. Smith thinks that there's a lot more to this phenomenon than the fact that superficial people like it when people stare at their Ferraris at stoplights. For if the poor are denied the recognition and respectability that even middle-class wealth brings, we then cannot but welcome a world that extends to as many people as possible an opportunity to better their condition, and thereby enjoy the respect and recognition essential to a life of dignity.

Whether our own world is such a world—whether the poorest among us today in fact have sufficient opportunities to better their condition—is a question that very much needs to be asked. But for our purposes, the main point is that Smith valued commercial society above all for its capacity to relieve poverty and to bring dignity to the lives of the least well-off. But at the same time, Smith was well aware that there is a darker side to all of this. And this dark side is especially evident when we consider what the connection of wealth to attention might mean for our efforts to live a life.

In short: Smith understood that wealth buys attention. But he also understood that the attention that wealth buys comes at a cost of its own. It particular, it often comes at the cost of other goods at least as important as attention—goods that are perhaps likely to seem even more important than attention to those who are self-consciously trying to live the best life possible. As it happens, this is a very big theme in Smith's work. But we can introduce it here by going back to something he said just above. Smith, as we saw, says that "wealth and greatness" are valued because they gratify our "love of distinction." But on the same page he also says that "wealth and greatness are mere trinkets of frivolous utility, no more adapted for procuring ease of body or tranquillity of mind than the tweezer-cases of the lover of toys." This will take some thinking through. Wealth gets us what our imaginations want. But it doesn't get us the "ease" our bodies want. Nor does it bring us the "tranquility" that our minds want. And if that's right, commercial life, it would seem, affords us some of what we need and want, but most certainly not all.

VI

--- ✶ ---

"The great source of both the misery and disorders of human life,
seems to arise from over-rating the difference between
one permanent situation and another."

*Or: unhappiness lies in over-valuing what we lack,
and under-valuing what we have.*

In chapter 5 we saw that bettering our condition can bring us
some but not all of what we need and want. It succeeds in
bringing us attention. But it fails to bring us ease of body and
tranquility of mind. But what if it turns out that things are
even worse? What if it turns out that in striving to better our
condition we're not simply trading off one good for others, but
are depriving ourselves of the possibility of ever enjoying those
other goods?

Smith goes a long way toward suggesting this in the quote
above. As we've seen, he thinks that the reason why we strive
to better our condition—why we work so hard to get ourselves
into a higher income bracket and raise our social standing—is
because we think that doing so will get us the attention that we
think will make us happy. But now it seems that it's not happiness and fulfillment that lies at the end of this road, but quite
the opposite—"misery" and "disorder"!

What on earth could Smith mean by this? To get our heads around this, we have to see that he's in fact making two discrete points here. The first concerns our propensity to over-value—or, as Smith says, "over-rate"—goods we don't currently have. This turns out to be another eminently familiar phenomenon. Anyone who has ever excitedly splurged on something but then found themselves bored by it a few months (or weeks or days or hours) later knows this all too well. Economists today like to use the example of lottery winners.[1] As it happens, people who buy lottery tickets dreaming that a big win will change their lives for the better all too often find out that actually winning causes disruption in their lives and often makes them less happy than they were before. But Smith knew all of this way back in 1759. "Avarice over-rates the difference between poverty and riches," he writes, "ambition, that between a private and a public station: vain-glory, that between obscurity and extensive reputation."[2] Up until now we've been led to believe that there is in fact a big difference between poverty and opulence, between obscurity and recognition. But maybe, Smith here suggests, there's not as big a difference between these as we may be inclined to think when we're caught up in our hopes and dreams for the future.

But over-rating the value of an imagined future state is only half of the issue here. The flip side is our propensity to under-value our present state. This is no less familiar to us all. It's a relatively rare person who consistently takes time out of her day to count all of her blessings and express her gratitude for the many gifts that we are all so lucky to have. Because, as it turns out, even the most ordinary among us have more or less all they need in order to be as happy as they could wish. Smith is explicit about this, telling us on the same page as our quote for this chapter that "in all the ordinary situations of human life, a well-disposed mind may be equally calm, equally cheerful, and equally contented."[3] He develops this even more powerfully on the following page, contrasting that "glittering and exalted situation" of our hopes and dreams with "our actual, though humble station." His point here is that it's only in the latter station that "our real happiness" is to be found, for "the pleasures of vanity and superiority are seldom consistent with perfect tranquillity, the principle and foundation of all real and satisfactory enjoyment."[4]

Smith drives this lesson home with an especially memorable parable that has left a deep impression on many readers of *The Theory of Moral Sentiments*. In the fourth part of the book he presents the cautionary tale of "the poor man's son, whom heaven in its anger has visited with ambition." This young man, "when he begins to look around him, admires the condition of the rich." He then starts to imagine what it might be like to have what they have, and as a result grows "enchanted with the distant idea of this felicity." And this in turn prompts him to do what he must in order to get it, and thus he "devotes himself for ever to the pursuit of wealth and greatness." The result is predictable to anyone who's been following Smith's argument so far. Working hard to get ahead, he submits himself "to more fatigue of body and more uneasiness of mind" than he ever could have known if he weren't a slave to his ambition. Pursuing this idea of a future felicity "which he may never arrive at," he thus "sacrifices a real tranquillity that is at all times in his power." And on his deathbed, all he can do is curse his ambition, and lament all those forgone pleasures that he "foolishly sacrificed for what, when he has got it, can afford him no real satisfaction."[5]

This is challenging stuff. It surely must have been for Smith's students at Glasgow who heard him present the early versions of his book in their philosophy class. It remains challenging stuff for my students today. When we read these passages, they too can't help but wonder if the remarkable quantities of time and energy they feel compelled to give to their own efforts to get ahead—studying and working and interning and networking and extracurricularing—is all going to be worth it for them in the end. It's a natural reaction, one that Smith seems to be trying to produce in us by telling the story this way. But what lesson does he hope we'll take away from all of this? How actually should we live our lives once we realize that "attention" might not be quite as good for us as our imaginations build it up to be?

It would be wrong, I think, to conclude from all of this that Smith's aim here is to get us simply to abandon the rat race and give up trying to better our condition altogether. He was too good an economist to think that would be good for society. After all, the economic growth that makes both opulence and the alleviation of poverty possible depends upon our acting on our natural desire to better our condition. At the same time, Smith clearly wants us to start thinking about how our efforts to better our condition can affect our individual happiness as well as the aggregate wealth of our society. The lesson of the poor man's son is that his particular way of trying to better his condition is good for his society but bad for his happiness. But putting things that way might lead us to wonder: are there other ways that we might go about bettering our condition— ways that might be both good for our society *and* good for ourselves?

And if so, what are they?

VII

———— ✴ ————

"Happiness and misery, which reside altogether in the mind,
must necessarily depend more upon the healthful or unhealthful,
the mutilated or entire state of the mind, than
upon that of the body."

Or: happiness lies within, and specifically in the healthy mind.

Adam Smith, we know, wrote two books, one on ethics and
one on economics. Given our interest in the question of what
it means to live a life, our primary focus in this book is naturally *The Theory of Moral Sentiments* rather than the *Wealth of
Nations*. But it would be surprising if it turned out that the
Wealth of Nations had no insights to offer into living a life—
after all, it's written by the same author (not to mention that
it's over a thousand pages). So what, if anything, does it have to
say to our question?

As it happens, it has quite a bit to say. That this is so is itself
noteworthy. For a long time, *The Theory of Moral Sentiments*
and the *Wealth of Nations* were seen as having little to do with
each other. One book, it was said, is about sympathy, while the
other book is about self-interest. This caused lots of ink to
be spilled on what a group of German scholars called *Das
Adam Smith Problem*: the problem of how (and whether)
the two books hang together. Scholars today, more aware of

the overlaps in the two books, generally don't still see this as a problem. But in this chapter I note another such overlap, one that concerns a key insight the *Wealth of Nations* has to offer with regard to the challenges of living life well.

That key insight, put simply and in the terms of the quotation for this chapter, is that happiness is less the result of our physical condition than our psychological condition. This insight turns out to be central to the idea of happiness that Smith develops in *The Theory of Moral Sentiments*, and in the chapters that follow we'll explore in detail Smith's idea of what a happy mind looks like. But for now we need to say a word or two about just how this idea maps onto Smith's economics, coming as it does in the *Wealth of Nations*. For here is where the idea starts becoming interesting. That happiness is a thing of the mind rather than the body isn't a revolutionary idea, after all; the Stoics argued this thousands of years ago, and mindfulness experts continue to emphasize it today. But what makes Smith's invocation of this idea so noteworthy is his understanding of its implications for our economic lives.

Smith specifically points to two such implications. First, Smith is aware, and indeed in ways we aren't often aware today, that the things that promote physical and bodily ease simply aren't enough for happiness. We today of course often act as if these sorts of things—what we sometimes call "creature comforts"—are sources of happiness. For example, for many years I've subscribed to the *Wall Street Journal*, and when the weekend edition comes I skip right to my favorite section: not "Business and Investing" (not this professor's forte), or even "Review" (which I always eventually read; it's excellent), but "Off Duty." "Off Duty" chronicles the latest trends in fashion and vacation spots and wines and gadgetry. Now, I'm not very tech-savvy, I have very little fashion sense, and I don't have a fancy wine cellar. But I adore "Off Duty," partly because it gives me something to talk about at parties, but mostly because it offers an unparalleled window onto how we in advanced commercial societies envision the accoutrements of the good life.

What would Smith have made of "Off Duty"? Surely it wouldn't have surprised him that an opulent culture would be so intrigued by such things. Smith himself (and in fact in the course of the story of the poor man's son, whom we met last chapter) called attention to the ways in which aspirants to the good life in commercial societies are often entranced by what he (quite derisively) calls "baubles and trinkets."[1] Yet what Smith, a founding father of capitalism, knew well—and what we, his heirs, often forget—is that even if these trinkets and baubles may bring us pleasure and comfort, happiness is something entirely different from pleasure and comfort. This partly explains his interest in the idea that it's the mind and not the body that determines our happiness.

Smith's insight into the difference between the body and the mind also has a second key implication for his economics. The context of the quote for this chapter is a discussion of education in Book 5 of the *Wealth of Nations*. This is important because in Book 5 Smith advances an argument that tends to surprise readers of the *Wealth of Nations* who know only Book 1 and its stories about the pin factory and the butcher and brewer and baker (to which we'll return below). These Book 1 stories are where Smith advances his famous claims about the superior productivity made possible by divided, specialized labor: arguably the key to his entire defense of commercial society.[2] But in Book 5, he makes clear that there's a human cost to all of this economic growth. For when specialized factory workers spend all their days doing one task over and over and over again, they not only get better at it (good for productivity, of course) but also get bored. And "bored" doesn't really begin to capture how bad the situation is; when Smith describes the mental state of these workers, he uses much more powerfully charged language: words like "mutilated" and "deformed" and "benumb" and "wretched."[3]

Thus Smith's paradox: the division of labor brings material opulence but also mental mutilation. What then ought we to do about this? Smith's response is that this "deserve[s] the most serious attention of government," and that the only thing that can remedy it is a comprehensive system of education, funded in part at public expense.[4] That's surprising enough coming from Smith; given his popular reputation, most today would expect him to be on the side of vouchers and charter schools. And these are far from the only institutions Smith recommends.[5] But what matters for our purposes is that this institutional solution to the problem of restoring the "healthful" and "entire" state of the mind—the solution that he emphasizes in the *Wealth of Nations*—is only one part of his response. For as Smith well knew, schools and other institutions can do only so much. What is also needed, and in the end what may be more important, is for us to reorient our thinking in such a way that we come to see our world and our activities in a new light. In particular, we need to rethink what our minds really need if they are to be maintained in their "healthful and entire state," along with a sense of just how the activities of our lives may move us closer to or further away from this goal.

VIII

─── ✶ ───

"Happiness consists in tranquillity and enjoyment. Without tranquillity there can be no enjoyment; and where there is perfect tranquillity there is scarce anything which is not capable of amusing."

Or: if we want to be happy, we first have to be at peace with ourselves.

Life today is busy. Busyness in fact largely seems to define our lives. Always on the move and always in a rush, we find ourselves constantly pulled in different directions, and afraid to take a break lest we fall behind forever. At the same time, and without any irony, we also say that all we want is to be happy. Why do we run to do all that we do? Because, we say, this is what we need to do in order to get what will make us happy. But our strange logic here suggests that we've all collectively missed the point of the tale of the poor man's son of chapter 6. For whatever else it may be, busyness clearly isn't the key to happiness. In fact, Smith thinks it's the opposite of happiness. For the truth is that "happiness consists in tranquillity and enjoyment."

This is another one of those moments in Smith's writings where he says something that is both obvious and not so obvious. The obvious point is that all of the running around that we do every day isn't good for us. We hope it is because we hope it will get us what we think we need to be happy. But the truth, Smith would have us know, is that real happiness lies not in getting a certain thing but in being a certain thing, in holding ourselves a certain way.

This requires in the first instance that we do less. When we try to do too much, we make ourselves miserable. Smith is explicit on this, insisting that most men's misfortunes "have arisen from their not knowing when they were well, when it was proper for them to sit still and to be contented."[1] All this mindless striving to better our condition rarely gets us what we hope it will, and usually just serves to make us miserable while we're doing it. Perhaps overstating his case, Smith even goes so far as to tell us that "in ease of body and peace of mind, all the different ranks of life are nearly upon a level, and the beggar, who suns himself by the side of the highway, possesses that security which kings are fighting for."[2]

I suspect that Smith's aim in writing this wasn't to try to get his readers to dedicate themselves to lives of begging. Given what he's said about poverty, that wouldn't seem a very promising path to happiness. But he does seem to be trying to get us to slow down a bit—to learn how to "sit still," as he says, and enjoy a little of the sun that shines down on the beggar but not those of us holed up in our offices. And that, I suspect, is a message that resonates with many of us. Amidst all our busyness today—and maybe because of all this busyness—people seem to be rededicating themselves to the project of rediscovering tranquility. A friend of mine has her iPhone programmed to chime every half hour so that she can remember to enjoy a "mindfulness minute." And everywhere we turn we see entire institutions dedicated to helping us regain our centers. From yoga studios to fitness gyms to meditation centers to acupuncture clinics, upper-middle-class America has created for itself a whole landscape of institutions to complement (or perhaps substitute for) all of the spaces—and especially houses of worship—to which human beings have traditionally gone for refuge from or transcendence of this world.

But all of this falls under the heading of the obvious that I mentioned above. There's nothing really all that profound or original about suggesting, as Smith does, that we can get and be much more if we simply try to have and do a little less. This is an important lesson, but it's also a fairly intuitive one. But what's not quite so obvious or intuitive are two other claims that are also at work here. And they need our attention since they strike right to the heart of the challenges involved in living a life, and maintaining a happy mind.

The first concerns Smith's suggestion that happiness consists not in tranquility alone, but in "tranquillity and enjoyment." This points to a somewhat different perspective on tranquility than one that might be more familiar from other traditions that likewise prize it. For example, in some schools of ancient philosophy and systems of religious monasticism, tranquility is found in asceticism—in renunciation of pleasures that distract us from our inner state and from higher goods. But this isn't Smith. By linking these two categories of tranquility and enjoyment together, he suggests we can't have one without the other. It isn't the case then that we can renounce enjoyment and still find happiness. Instead, if we hope to do justice to the full range of our natures, we have to find a way of living that brings tranquility and enjoyment together—a way of living that strikes a middle path between the ascetic who deprives himself of enjoyment in search of tranquility and the poor man's son who deprives himself of tranquility in search of enjoyment.

Put differently: tranquility is where our happiness lies, but the tranquility that will make us truly happy is the tranquility that is suited to beings like us who seek enjoyment. And this in turn leads to a second less obvious but important claim at work here. The sort of tranquility best suited to us must also be a tranquility that squares with another side of our natures, and specifically our natures as active beings. Above we saw that Smith thinks we are fundamentally active creatures: "man was made for action." But that raises certain challenges when it comes to tranquility. It's easy to think of the tranquil state as a passive state. When we call to mind the monk or the sage we imagine a person at rest, apart from the world. And Smith himself even perpetuates a bit of this stereotype: to say that we need to "sit still" and enjoy the sunshine itself suggests that what we need is less movement and more stillness and quiet. But if Smith is right, and we are at the end of the day beings who have been made to act and to be in motion, exactly what sort of "tranquility" is suited to us? Smith is evidently after something very different from the tranquility of either the monk in his cloister or the philosopher in her study. And it's here that we begin to see that Smith is very self-consciously asking one of the most difficult questions about the life best suited to us. For if we need tranquility to be happy, and if indeed the tranquility of withdrawal from the world is unavailable to us, exactly what sort of tranquility should we as active creatures seek?

IX

---- ✳ ----

"This disposition to admire, and almost to worship, the rich and the powerful, and to despise, or, at least, to neglect persons of poor and mean condition, though necessary both to establish and to maintain the distinction of ranks and the order of society, is, at the same time, the great and most universal cause of the corruption of our moral sentiments."

Or: capitalism brings material benefits,
but it also has moral costs our lives must address.

Adam Smith had a unique ability to see both sides of an issue. This makes him very different from how we today tend to grapple with issues. We today live in a polarized age. Our social and political discussions are not so much debates as they are ideological boxing matches in which each side rushes out of its far corner swinging at its opponent. And not only are our debates dominated by combativeness and ideological extremism, but our very beliefs and opinions tend to be formed in spaces where we don't have a chance to hear the other side. Political scientists today call these "echo chambers" and philosophers call them "epistemic bubbles." But the idea is the same: our beliefs are shaped by engaging with only a single side with which we are already disposed to agree, and to which we merely become more attached as a result. But not Smith. He is committed to seeing both sides, even on the issues dearest to him.[1] So when it comes to the issue of capitalism, he tells us forthrightly: the same dispositions that promote the "order of society" are at once "the great and most universal cause of the corruption of our moral sentiments."

I suspect that there might be more to learn from this line than any other line in the whole of *The Theory of Moral Sentiments*. In the first place, Smith here gives us an example of what it looks like to engage in mature and productive debate, even on issues that we feel passionately about. So far from giving us only the side of the story that best fits with his preferred narrative and preferred conclusion, he wants us to see both sides of the story of capitalism, its material benefits as well as its moral costs. This commitment to balance and to telling the whole truth of the matter makes Smith worth reading today. But there is also a substantive point here that he wants to convey, and it's on this that we need to focus as it strikes at the heart of the challenges of living life well.

The challenges, as I see them, are twofold. Both are the result of "this disposition to admire, and almost to worship, the powerful." We've seen this disposition at work already of course: it's what drives the poor man's son (and all of us who have ever experienced the ambition and desire for recognition that drives the poor man's son) to do all he does. But now we can see that this disposition, the desire to emulate the rich and follow in their path, comes at two very specific costs. The first concerns its effect on us as individuals. As we've already seen, our frantic pursuit of attention and distinction comes at an enormous psychic cost as it forces us to sacrifice the tranquility needed for happiness. For even as we pursue the incentives that our world rewards, we are led ever further away from what it is that our minds need. In some deep sense then there's a discord between what our world wants us to want and what our beings in fact need. Living our lives well requires that we figure out a productive way to navigate this divide between what the world says is good and what is in fact genuinely good for us.

There's also a second challenge here. Where the first involved the way in which our world transforms our relationships with ourselves, this second challenge involves the way our world transforms our relationships with others. Our propensity to admire the rich, in short, doesn't just alienate us from ourselves. It also alienates us from those around us. And even this language of "alienation"—a language we have inherited from Karl Marx, himself one of Smith's readers—doesn't quite capture what Smith is after. For it's not just that we are somehow distant or estranged from others as a result of worshipping wealth. As Smith tells us, this worship is much more sinister in its effects, as it leads us to "neglect" and even to "despise" the least well-off among us. In saying this, Smith goes even further than he had before. In previous chapters we saw how the attention we pay to the rich leads us to avert our eyes from the poor. But now it seems that our benign neglect isn't all that far removed from active hostility and contempt. And if that's so, the effect of living in a society like ours, one that rewards our efforts to better our condition, is that both our relationship with ourselves and our relationship with others are transformed for the worse. For just as our pursuit of attention distances us from the ease of body and the tranquility of mind that we are led by nature to seek, so too our focus on attention encourages us to "neglect" and "despise" others in ways that are in obvious tension with those "principles of our nature," as described in that crucial first line of *The Theory of Moral Sentiments*, that lead us to take an "interest" in others and to regard their happiness as "necessary" to us.

And this brings us to the heart of the problem with regard to living a life. Smith's worry is that the world into which we have all been born, even as it affords us certain great and genuine goods, changes us and changes how we relate to others. It is a worry that at least some of us today likely share. And it was certainly a worry shared by at least one of Smith's contemporaries. Three years after the publication of the first edition of *The Theory of Moral Sentiments*, the Genevan philosopher Jean-Jacques Rousseau—a thinker Smith had read and translated, and with whom he agreed on many (though hardly all) points—would publish a remarkable work that grappled with many of the same questions Smith addresses in his book. This book—Rousseau's *Emile, or On Education*—told the story of the education of a young man by his tutor, spanning the period from his birth to his wedding. Rousseau's aim in writing it was to offer an account of what it would look like to raise what he called "a natural man in society." Now, what exactly Rousseau meant by that has been the subject of many studies.[2] But for our purposes what matters is that at least part of what is at stake in this project is a worry that Rousseau shared with Smith. As Rousseau explains, our modern world poses certain specific challenges to our efforts to live well, as it puts us in tension with ourselves and with others:

> From these contradictions is born the one we constantly experience within ourselves. Swept along in contrary routes by nature and by men, forced to divide ourselves between these different impulses, we follow a composite impulse which leads us to neither one goal nor the other. Thus, in conflict and floating during the whole course of our life, we end it without having been able to put ourselves in harmony with ourselves and without having been good either for ourselves or for others.[3]

Rousseau's project in *Emile* is to discover a means by which we might recapture the unity imperiled by the pressures of our modern world, and thereby rediscover a way to live that can, as he says, render us at once good for ourselves and good for others. It is precisely this same project that lies at the heart of *The Theory of Moral Sentiments*, which, like *Emile*, aims to show us how we might live well in light of both the divisions of our nature and the challenges of our world.

And with that in mind, we now need to make a shift from diagnosing the problem to solving it. So what then does Smith think we should do if we hope to live lives that are good and useful to both others and ourselves?

X

"The mind, therefore, is rarely so disturbed, but that the company of a friend will restore it to some degree of tranquillity and sedateness."

Or: we are not made to be alone, evident in that friendship promotes our tranquility.

Having defined the chief challenges to living a life in the modern world, Smith must now turn to the question of how we can best meet these challenges. So what is to be done? Quite a bit, in fact. And much of it will be both intellectually and personally demanding. Yet Smith's advice on this front begins with some basic lessons, close to home. One of the most important is the recommendation of friendship that he gives in the quote above. Have you lost your tranquility? Do you feel anxious? If so, get out of the house and find your friends.

It's simple enough advice. When we're wrapped up in ourselves, especially in ways that cause us anxiety and worry, friendship can offer us an escape from ourselves. When we're with others, we can be in some sense less with ourselves, or at least less exclusively with ourselves. This idea that friendship is good because it draws us out beyond ourselves will reappear in Smith's recommendations of other practices later, as we'll see. Yet for now the key idea is that friendship is useful insofar as it helps restore the tranquility necessary for happiness. And not only tranquility. We saw above that happiness requires not just tranquility, but enjoyment. But friends provide this too, Smith thinks. For when we rejoice with our friends, "their joy literally becomes our joy," and "our heart swells and overflows with real pleasure."[1]

Smith's ideal friendship thus involves a mutual sharing of joy. This is important for two reasons. First, for Smith friendship is a two-way street. Appreciating this can help us to guard against a possible misinterpretation of the quote for this chapter. To say that the presence of our friends can help us relieve our anxiety and regain our tranquility runs the risk of reducing friendship to instrumentality—a good we value only for the self-interested reason that it gets us something we want. Friendship of course does do this, but it doesn't only do this. For after all, if we approach friendship with this instrumental mind-set, we'll never get what we want out of it anyway. Friendship of the sort that Smith describes is based not simply around taking, but around sharing. Yes, it brings us tranquility, but we can get this tranquility that is so good for ourselves only if we first open ourselves up to receive and share and rejoice in the joy of others, for no other reason than the fact that it is their joy.

This notion of sharing also offers a window into a second crucial aspect of Smith's concept of friendship. This concerns the activities properly characteristic of friends. What exactly do friends do together? All kinds of activities might come to mind. Some are more solitary and involve two friends doing the same thing next to each other at the same time: imagine two friends dining together, or running together, or fishing together. All of these activities may be more enjoyable for being done in the presence of a friend, but they can also all be done alone. This makes them different from the sorts of activities that can be done only with others. Imagine two friends making music together, playing tennis together, or having a discussion together. These activities are different insofar as they are activities in which the mutual engagement of the two friends together creates something or makes possible something that couldn't come to be, at least in the same way, if the friends were apart. And it's this second sort of friendship that Smith most values. The sort of friendship that restores our tranquility, he explains, requires this sharing of a deeper sort. This is why he calls "society and conversation" the "most powerful remedies for restoring the mind to its tranquillity" as well as useful means of preserving the temper that is "so necessary to self-satisfaction and enjoyment."[2] Conversation, the sharing of thoughts and words, may be the most intimate sort of sharing for friends, and the activity best suited to them.

We know what friends should do (converse) and we know what friends get out of this (tranquility and enjoyment). But one last question regarding friendship needs to be addressed: namely, what kind of person should we choose for our friend? Who makes the best friend? Smith has a pretty direct answer to this: "the attachment which is founded upon the love of virtue, as it is certainly, of all attachments, the most virtuous; so it is likewise the happiest, as well as the most permanent and secure." If we hope to reap all the goods that good friendship can bring, we do best to choose the best people for our friends. This itself has a further happy effect. For these sorts of friendships need not be limited to one other, Smith insists, "but may safely embrace all the wise and virtuous, with whom we have been long and intimately acquainted."[3] Now, Smith needs to do some more to help us understand what it means to be devoted to "the love of virtue." He also needs to explain what it is that makes these "wise and virtuous" people so wise and virtuous. But even now he's helped us recognize that as we go about the task of living our lives, it's not good for us to be alone.

XI

———— ✴ ————

"Man is an anxious animal and must have his care swept off
by something that can exhilarate the spirits."

*Or: life's simple pleasures are also good for us,
but only in moderation and with self-command.*

With this chapter I have to ask for your indulgence, and indeed in two senses. First, the quotation for this chapter is the
only one in this book that doesn't come directly from Smith's
own hand. Instead it comes from a set of notes taken by one of
the students in his jurisprudence course. Now, as any teacher
will tell you, what we say when we lecture and what our
students actually take away from our lectures aren't always
the same. So we have to take these student notes with a grain
of salt.

But I also have to ask your indulgence in a second sense, as
the quotation concerns a subject a little less heady than the big
themes of virtue and happiness on which we've been focusing.
In fact, the quotation turns out to be *about* indulgence: specifically drinking. Now if Smith's students were anything like
students today, it's not surprising that their ears may have
perked up at Smith's alcohol reference. What's interesting for
us is that Smith himself was interested in drinking. And as it
turns out, he was interested in it for reasons central to his

economics and his ethics, and indeed to his conception of what it means to live a life.

On the economic front, Smith presents the quote for our chapter as an illustration of the potential dangers of certain kinds of government intervention, especially taxation. The main focus of his discussion is the relationship between a commodity's "natural price" and its "market price," and his key argument here is that anything that "keeps goods above their natural price" for any length of time "diminishes a nation's opulence." Now of course lots of different factors affect a commodity's price, taxes being one among many. But Smith here focuses on the way in which taxes on "beer, or whatever is the strong drink of the country" often raise the price of alcohols above what ordinary people can afford, with the result that "the society lives less happy when only the few can possess them."[1]

But it's not just society as a whole that is less happy as a result. Smith also thinks that these sorts of policies negatively impact individual happiness. And this is where his argument starts moving closer to the themes that lie at the heart of this book. Ultimately the reason why taxes on alcohol are unwise isn't that such taxes make society less happy (though they do) or because such taxes fail to curb excessive consumption (Smith insists that they in fact do tend to fail on this front), but because such taxes do violence to our basic nature as human beings. "Man is an anxious animal," he tells his students. We are, that is, by nature creatures with certain psychological needs—creatures with "cares" that "must" be "swept off." This is an arresting statement about human nature. To say that "man is an anxious animal," as Smith does here, is to take a considerable step beyond what Aristotle famously said when he said that "man is a political animal."[2] At the risk of saying too little at a point where so much more needs to be said, almost all of the difference between Smith and Aristotle, and between ancient and modern political thought, is encapsulated here.

But ultimately the reason why the quotation for this chapter matters for us is for what it has to say about living a life, and especially the challenges that anxiety poses to our efforts to live well. Overcoming anxiety and preserving tranquility of course aren't all we need for a good life. At the same time, it might not be possible for us to live well if we don't take care of this first. As such, we'd be wise, Smith thinks, to take advantage of all the resources at our disposal that can help move us in this direction. In the previous chapter, we saw that friends are one important such resource. In the next chapter we'll see that our efforts to feel less anger and to feel more love can pay off on this front. But for now Smith's suggestion is that a drink can help too. It's a suggestion that resonates with me—and not just because I like good beer and bourbon. It resonates because it reminds me that Smith, amidst all his appreciation of the big themes of life (virtue, duty, perfection, happiness, etc.), was deeply sensitive to the ways in which our ordinary human activities and behaviors are also part of living life well—including such ordinary activities as drinking and socializing.

That said, let's never forget: Smith recommended drinking, but he also did so very much as a lover of virtue and as a professor of moral philosophy. As a result, maybe not surprisingly, the drinking he recommends is most certainly very moderate drinking. Smith knew well that the pleasures of the body "often mislead us into many weaknesses which we afterwards have much reason to be ashamed of." Partly as a result, Smith recommends the key virtue of "self-command." Now, self-command can take many forms, and it often has to do with noble and heroic acts. But it also is what lies at the heart of the virtue Smith called "temperance"—that "command of those appetites of the body" that serves "to confine them within those limits, which grace, which propriety, which delicacy, and modesty, require."[3]

I have a mentor who, over dinner, once commented to the table that moderation, as Aristotle envisioned it, isn't zero martinis, or two martinis, but one martini. Aristotle and Smith may have had their differences, but on this point, I think, they'd agree.

XII

———— ✳ ————

"Hatred and anger are the greatest poison to the happiness
of a good mind."

*Or: tranquility is threatened by hatred and anger,
but promoted by gratitude and love.*

In chapter 10 we saw that one thing Smith thinks we can do to preserve or regain our tranquility is to be with our friends. Yet tranquility and thus happiness demand not only that we do certain things, but that we hold ourselves in a certain way. This means that we can't simply try to escape ourselves by surrounding ourselves with others; instead we also need to order ourselves—to organize ourselves in such a way that on the whole we feel more of some feelings and less of others.

The sorts of feelings that we need to try to minimize are what Smith calls "unsocial passions." Foremost among these are hatred and anger. These have been given to us for a reason, and they certainly have a social and political utility (as we'll see in a moment). But they're also inimical to the happiness of an individual. "There is, in the very feeling of those passions," Smith explains, "something harsh, jarring, and convulsive, something that tears and distracts the breast, and is altogether destructive of that composure and tranquillity of mind which is so necessary to happiness."[1] Hatred and anger thus aren't just bad for those to whom such feelings are directed; they're also bad for those who have to feel them. So in some deep sense, hatred and anger are both bad for others and bad for us ourselves.

The opposite is true of the feelings that are the opposite of hatred and anger. If we really want to achieve the composure and tranquility that are so necessary to happiness, we need to recognize that these are "best promoted by the contrary passions of gratitude and love." For just as hatred and anger are painful to both those to whom they are directed and those who are so unhappy as to feel them, love and gratitude bring joy to both those to whom they're directed and those who experience them firsthand. And that love has this power Smith leaves no doubt, explaining that "the sentiment of love is, in itself, agreeable to the person who feels it," as it "soothes and composes the breast, seems to favour the vital motions, and to promote the healthful state of the human constitution."[2] Love then is good not just for the beloved, but also (and perhaps especially) for the lover. In this way love and gratitude play central roles in Smith's vision of living life well. As we have already had occasion to note, Smith's master question when it comes to living life well is that we need to discover a way of living that is at once good for others and good for ourselves. And love and gratitude are perhaps the preeminent sentiments that are at once good for others and good for ourselves.

Of course, Smith still needs to explain what exactly he means by "love" here. When we think of love today we tend to think of romantic love. Smith himself has some things to say about romantic love, to be sure, and not all of them are charitable.[3] But for us, the key point is that when he speaks of love in the sort of way he does here, he has in mind the love of others we sometimes call charity, or neighbor love. Also, Smith needs to show us what exactly a life driven by this charity or neighbor love will look like. But we've taken a crucial step here, and at the very least we've seen that the task of living our lives well challenges us to live in such a way that our lives are lives of love.

That said, before going too much further, I need to add a brief caveat to something I said above. We noted above that Smith thinks hatred and anger are "destructive." That's true for most of *The Theory of Moral Sentiments*. But there's also a crucial exception to this rule. In one place Smith argues that hatred and anger, felt in a certain way toward certain persons as a result of certain acts, are not destructive but constructive. This is the specific form of hatred or anger he calls "sympathetic indignation" or "sympathetic resentment."[4] This is the hatred or anger that good people instinctively feel when they see the innocent and weak hurt by the selfish and strong. A young man assaults an old woman to steal her purse: any person of ordinary decency who has the misfortune to see this can't help but feel a visceral indignation toward the young man, and a desire that he pay a price for what he's so unjustly done. This desire for vengeance may not bring us pleasure, and it certainly doesn't promote our tranquility or enjoyment, at least in the short term. At the same time, this instinctive desire for vengeance is what leads us to support those institutions of justice that bring order to society. So hatred or anger of this sort may be painful for a good person to experience, but it is clearly good for society that we do experience it—perhaps in the same way that the ambition of the poor man's son may be inimical to his tranquility but yet beneficial for the order of society.

But that's an exception (even if a crucial exception) to Smith's general rule. And this general rule is a simple one, and maybe even a deceptively simple one. Want to be happy? Want others around you to be happy? Feel less hate, and more love. I think this is in fact a message central to Smith's vision of what it means to live life well. At the same time, if this were all Smith were saying, he wouldn't be much of a philosopher. Put as simply as I put it just now, a bumper sticker could suffice for his book. But bumper-sticker wisdom, even if it can help distill some of Smith's core claims into a form that we can readily get our minds around, hardly captures what matters in *The Theory of Moral Sentiments*. For what Smith so far hasn't yet done—and what he needs a book like *The Theory of Moral Sentiments* in order to do—is explain how exactly we can come to hate less and love more. If indeed love is both good for others and good for ourselves, what must we do if we hope to become move loving?

XIII

———— ✶ ————

"Humanity does not desire to be great, but to be beloved."

Or: at the end of the day, what we most want is love.

We like to love—this much we know from the previous chapter. As we saw there, the experience of loving others is good for us. In Smith's own words, love is an "agreeable" feeling, and promotes our "healthful" state. But it turns out that love is also good for us in a second way. For not only is it good for us to love, it's also good for us to be loved. Thus the claim at the heart of the quote above: ultimately what we most want isn't the greatness that we so often sweat and scurry after, but love.

At this point, we can see just how complex Smith's views on so-called "self-interest" in fact are. We started our inquiry by examining his claim that we have a natural interest in securing the goods of the body. We then saw that we also have, thanks to our imaginations, an interest in the attention of others. We followed this by noting that beyond all of this, we have an interest in securing the tranquility of mind without which we can't be happy. But having now broached the topic of love, Smith reveals that all that's come before has been in some sense provisional, mere anticipations of what it is that truly defines "humanity." And thus his point here that a distinguishing characteristic of humanity is the desire for love.

Now, I suspect that all this talk of love is likely to make some readers uncomfortable. Lots of people appeal to Smith—and Smith himself appeals to lots of people—for what they hope to find in him: celebration of the rough-and-tumble life of competition in the world of the free market, where the strong succeed and the feeble fail. Love doesn't seem to have any place in that world. That said, there are economists out there who contest this view of the market, and who seek, as it were, to bring love back in.[1] It's a position to which I'm not unsympathetic. But I'm focused here on a different claim—namely that Smith believed that the experience of love and being loved is essential to the sort of happiness appropriate for us as human beings. He indeed tells us this in several places. "There is a satisfaction in the consciousness of being beloved," he thus explains early in his book, "which, to a person of delicacy and sensibility, is of more importance to happiness, than all the advantage which he can expect to derive from it."[2] Just a few pages later he repeats the lesson even more succinctly, telling us "the chief part of human happiness arises from the consciousness of being beloved."[3]

I noted above that some readers may balk at all of this love talk. Others, I suspect, will welcome it. But both types of readers may wonder whether this love talk isn't showing Smith to be a little schizophrenic, and maybe even in contradiction with himself. After all, earlier he said that we want attention. Now he says we want love. How do these things go together? So too earlier he said that happiness requires tranquility and enjoyment. Now he says that the "chief part" of happiness comes from love. What's going on here?

This is a serious question, and demands a response much longer than anything I can give here. Suffice it to say, for now, that part of the art of reading Smith closely and indeed philosophically consists in figuring out how all of his different claims go together, even (and maybe especially) when they don't seem to match up perfectly on their face. I have a friend who likes to say that when he reads *The Theory of Moral Sentiments* it often feels like Smith "giveth on one page, and taketh away on another." That rings true, and in the end, I think a lot of the fun of reading Smith lies in patiently trying to figure out how all the moving parts build off of one another and ultimately hang together into one integrated system.

But that's something that I'll leave you to discover on your own when you tackle *The Theory of Moral Sentiments* directly. Given our focus here on Smith's insights into living life well, I want to make two other points. One concerns what Smith is up to in calling attention to both our desires for attention and our desires for love. At least one thing he wants to do in framing the issue this way, and setting these different objects of self-interest next to each other, is to prompt us to compare these goods and to make our own judgments about their value. Attention and love, after all, share a lot in common. When felt by others toward us, they both represent feelings of affection. Yet ultimately their differences may eclipse their similarities. Attention, as Smith has explained, is something we often get from others because we have something that they want. We get attention because we have certain goods—wealth, fame, status—that those who attend to us lack and wish they had. But love, whatever else it may be, isn't the same. We love those we love for who and what they are, not for what they have. Attention and love are thus expressed for very different reasons. And it may be that they are also desired for very different reasons, and indeed desired differently by different types of people.

This latter point is one that we'll need to circle back to in a few chapters. For now though I'd like to close with a question prompted by the way that Smith, in the lines we've examined in this chapter, describes love. The love of others, as we've seen, is something that Smith thinks we want, and indeed need to have, if we hope to be happy. How then do we get this love? What must we be or become if we seek to be loved? Perhaps even more importantly, given the fact that we are after all beings made for action, what exactly must we *do* if we hope to be loved?

XIV

———— ✳ ————

"Kindness is the parent of kindness; and if to be beloved by our brethren be the great object of our ambition, the surest way of obtaining it is, by our conduct to show that we really love them."

Or: it is the act of loving that brings us love in return.

We ended the last chapter with a question. If we want to be loved by others, what do we need to do in order to get others to give us the love we long for? Here Smith offers his answer. We get love—which, he here suggests, may in fact be "the great object of our ambition"—when we give love. And we give love only when we love actively. Thoughts and words are not enough; it is only through our "conduct" that we "show that we really love" others.

On the face of things, all of this talk of love seems far removed from the world of the market. That world, as we've already had occasion to note, is the world of competition and self-interest. But in a crucial sense what Smith is describing here is very much a part of this world. It's true that the good that he's describing, love, isn't one we tend to associate with market transactions (except maybe those of a very particular sort). But the process that he describes here is easily recognizable as an exchange transaction. Smith signals this by his language, making clear that this process is quite literally one in which we seek to "obtain," by the surest means possible, the good that is most dear to us. Love is here just the coin of the realm, and Smith's point is simply that in order to get the love we want, we need to give some love in return.

In putting matters this way, Smith brings us directly into the world of exchange that he famously describes in the *Wealth of Nations*. There's a well-known passage early in the *Wealth of Nations* that always gets trotted out when someone wants to make the case that there's no place for the mushy sentiment of benevolence in the harsh world of the market. Here we're notoriously told that "it is not from the benevolence of the butcher, the brewer, or the baker, that we expect our dinner, but from their regard to their own interest." That has seemed to some as all the proof that's needed for Dr. Stigler's case that self-interest is the "granite" on which Smith's system is built. But if we look just up that same page, we see that Smith is less concerned to make value judgments here than simply to describe what's going on when two people get together to exchange goods. The thought behind exchange, as he puts it, is "give me that which I want, and you shall have this which you want."[1] But something quite like this is happening in a lover hoping to be loved in return (though with the caveat that a lover hoping to be loved is often more like what game theory calls a first mover: she doesn't ask for love promising love in return, but loves first).

I emphasize all of this for several reasons. First and foremost, there's a key lesson that Smith conveys here to those interested in the question of how to live a life. For if Smith is right that at the end of the day what we most want is to be loved, he's here given us the most explicit advice anyone seeking this good could ask for. This then is one of those places in Smith's work where he shifts from simply describing how it is that people tend to act to telling them how they should act if they want to live well. Smith specialists like to debate whether Smith is ultimately best understood as a social scientist whose goal is to describe human behavior objectively, or as more of a normative thinker—that is, someone who recommends certain types of behavior as in fact preferable to others. My own view is that we can't understand all Smith says if we read him exclusively through the first, more scientific lens.[2] This of course isn't the place to hash all this out. For now, the point to be made is that Smith has much to say to readers with normative interests, and that this is one place where this comes through.

This leads to a second point. Smith, I think, believes that there are better ways and worse ways to act. Relatedly, he also thinks that there are better and worse ways to live. If we deny this, I don't think we can make sense of much of what he says about either virtue or happiness. At the same time, we need to be very careful here. Just because Smith thinks that there are better and worse ways to live, we shouldn't assume he thinks there is a single best way for all people to live. This approach was common in ancient philosophy, in which the idea of "the best life" for a human being was often invoked—the one life that all seeking to live as good a life as possible should aspire to. But that isn't Smith. Smith is instead what we today sometimes call a "pluralist."[3] That is, even though he thinks there are better and worse ways to live, he never argues that there is a single best way for everyone to live.

This makes Smith's approach especially valuable today, I think. Smith pushes back against a one-size-fits-all approach to human excellence, arguing instead that different types of excellence are suited to different sorts of people. Here he's focused on those who take love as "the great object of their ambition." But we also know that there are of course people who take attention for the object of their ambition. An ancient philosopher might have simply written off attention lovers as hopelessly lost. But Smith, even as he knows that it would be foolish to try to convert the attention lovers into love lovers, still thinks that we can show both the love lovers and the attention lovers better and worse ways to pursue the respective objects of their ambitions. And this is where the virtue of prudence enters. In a key chapter in part 6 of *The Theory of Moral Sentiments*, Smith describes the character of the person that he calls "the prudent man." The prudent man is in many ways the antidote to the poor man's son, as the prudent man shows us a better way to go about bettering our condition than the poor man's son in his desperate headlong rush forward. The prudent man is after the same good as the poor man's son; he too looks forward to his condition "growing better and better every day." But he goes about it differently, working slowly and gradually; Smith especially emphasizes "the steadiness of his industry" and "the regularity of his temperance." The contrast with the poor man's son is clear. Both work to advance their self-interest, but where one does so desperately, obsessively, and impatiently, the other one does so in a way that both enables him to better his condition and also brings him "secure tranquillity."[4]

This brings me to the last point that I want to make in this chapter. The love lovers Smith here describes are people driven by a need to be loved. They love not because they think that it is just the right thing to do—the sort of thing they'd do even if they knew they would never be loved back. On the contrary, their acts of love are driven by their desire to get love in return. For them love is a reward, something they hope others will reciprocate. But that's very different from how many other schools of thought have understood love. In particular, Christianity—a religion Smith himself again and again and again identifies as a religion of love (we'll come back to this in chapter 27)—is often taken to regard love as the opposite of self-interest: "disinterested love" or "selfless love" has been the goal of many Christians. Now, many debates have been held over this concept both within the church and beyond, but for us it leads us to wonder: given all Smith has said about love as something we give because it's something we hope to get, can there be any place in his system for another sort of love, a love that loves without hope of recompense?

XV

"All the members of human society stand in need of each others
assistance, and are likewise exposed to mutual injuries. Where the
necessary assistance is reciprocally afforded from love,
from gratitude, from friendship, and esteem, the
society flourishes and is happy."

*Or: we need others' help, but it's only when we all get and
give love that society flourishes.*

We know from the last chapter that if we hope to get the love
of others, we first have to give them our love. Individual human
happiness depends on this. But what if this activity wasn't
limited to just a few individuals? What if everyone loved each
other and was loved by them in return? It seems so idyllic. Can
you even imagine such a world? Adam Smith could, as it happens. For this is precisely what he describes in the quotation
above: a world in which everyone provides "assistance" to each
other, an assistance "reciprocally afforded from love."

This is the moment that Mr. Gekko and his friends, if
they've even bothered to stick around this long, go running for
the exits. They can't be bothered with this sort of stuff, the sort
of thing that idealistic visionaries dream up—imagined uto-
pias that never existed, and never will exist. Why waste a minute of our time, they ask, on things that aren't real? Now, that's

a serious question, especially for us. I started this book by trying to induce a bit of urgency, calling to the forefront of our minds that uncomfortable though obvious truth that we each have only a single life to live, a life that is surely going by much faster than any of us might wish. So the question of why we should spend precious time thinking about an imaginary ideal likely isn't a question on the minds of the Gekko gang only, but is also on the minds of decent people concerned to live the best life possible.

In response, I suggest there are at least three reasons why we should take Smith's vision seriously. The first concerns the simple fact of its fundamental distance from our world today, the real world we all inhabit. Our world, as everyone knows, is a world that is famously "divided" and "fractured" and "split." But Smith's vision is the exact opposite. It's a world, as he says in the next sentence, in which "all the different members" are "bound together by the agreeable bands of love and affection," and are "drawn to one common centre of mutual good offices."[1] This is a world then that has a "common center" of gravity, a unifying point around which all its "different members" can come together and not just coexist but coalesce. And perhaps most importantly, what makes this possible is "love and affection." Where competition for attention drives people apart, expressions of affection and love bring them together. There are surely more than a few lessons here for those who wonder just what it is going to take to heal the wounds and divisions of our world today.

A second reason why we should take Smith seriously here concerns the implications of this vision for our master question of living a life. The quote for this chapter describes a certain vision of the good society. As such, it is properly a contribution to social or political philosophy. Of course our own master question is not really political but ethical, a question of moral philosophy, not political philosophy. But even though we try to disaggregate these disciplines when we talk about sub-specialties in professional academic life today, when it comes to the question of living life well it's clear that there can't be any such readily demarcated boundaries. The key issue here is that we don't live our lives in bubbles; living a life requires a matrix in which life is to be lived. And presumably the project of living a good life will be facilitated by living in a good matrix. Now, I don't want to go too far on this front. These are deep waters in political philosophy, and we have enough on our plate as it is. But in formulating his vision of the good society as he has—and specifically by explicitly identifying this good society as the society that is "flourishing and happy"—Smith invites us to wonder whether this society might be advantageous to or even necessary for living a life that is flourishing and happy.

To these two reasons for taking Smith's vision seriously let me add a third. As we've seen, Gekko and his fellow cynics don't have time to mess about with ideals. We need, they say, to use our time thinking about what's possible and what paths are actually available to us, rather than what's impossible and unavailable to us. To my mind, that's hardly a silly position. When it comes to making real-world choices, whether about the kind of society we want to create or about the kind of life we want to lead, we as human beings will always face certain limits on the range of our choices. So let's grant that in fact our range of choices in the real world is indeed limited by the constraints of the real world and the constraints of the way we've been made. At the same time, however appealing such realism may be, this line of thinking runs into a problem. The problem is that even though our range of choices may be limited, we still have to make a choice—we still need to choose one sort of society or one sort of life over another, since we can't have them all. But how do we make such a choice? How do we know what path to follow?

Here's where the idea of the ideal comes in. When we imagine an ideal, and fix it in our minds, we have something to aim at. An ideal of this sort gives us a sense of where we want to go, and even gives us a way to measure whether or not the path that we've chosen to take is getting us closer to where we want to go. In this way, ideals are useful even (and maybe especially) to realists, as they help us organize our choices and rank different options by how they measure up. The danger of course comes when we fool ourselves into thinking that we can finally and fully realize our ideal in the real world. Herein lies the path to perdition and perhaps even political chaos. Yet I'm fairly confident that Smith never suffered from that sort of naïveté.

Smith himself offers a memorable excoriation of the sort of visionary that he calls "the man of system." This is the sort of politician who is "so enamoured with the supposed beauty of his own ideal plan of government" that he thinks he can arrange the lives of real people "with as much ease as the hand arranges the different pieces upon a chess-board." Smith knows that denying freedom can only lead to disaster, which is why he so vigorously defends the superiority of free societies governed by invisible hands to arranged societies manipulated by the hands of system-men. But for all that, he knows that it's also the case that we can't do without ideals altogether. It's for this reason that he insists that "some general, and even systematical, idea of the perfection of policy and law, may no doubt be necessary for directing the views of the statesman."[2] And not only in politics. As we'll see later, not only political life but also moral life requires that we fix in our minds an "idea of perfection," even when we know—and indeed must never forget—that as human beings we can never attain this perfection in reality.

In any case, I think this explains what Smith is up to here. In the paragraph that follows, he describes a very different society, one built around "a mercenary exchange of good offices according to an agreed valuation."[3] This of course sounds a lot like the society he describes in the *Wealth of Nations*—a society built on the reciprocal exchange of goods and services rather than the bonds of affection and love.[4] And given the fact that Smith wrote a whole long book about that market society, how much should we really make of his account of the society of love? Was he just trying to do some ground clearing, sweeping away the visionary dream before getting about his study of what's possible? We would, I think, do Smith a disservice to see it that way. Smith after all goes out of his way to tell us that this second society, the one that lacks "mutual love and affection," is "less happy and agreeable." It will never flourish, he says, but only "subsist."[5] I suppose some people might be fine with this; subsisting after all is better than chaos. But I suspect that if you've gotten this far in this book, you're probably not one of those people. To we who care about human flourishing and even would like to flourish in our own right—Smith asks a different question: what do we need to do if we hope to bring our actual society closer, even if just a little bit, to becoming a society that flourishes and is happy?

XVI

"Man naturally desires, not only to be loved, but to be lovely."

Or: we don't just want to get love; we also want to be someone who deserves it.

I mentioned above my friend's line about how Smith gives on one page and takes away on another. This is a pretty common feeling among careful readers of his work: just when you think you've heard everything he has to say about some topic, suddenly he adds one last little point—which then forces you to rethink everything you thought you knew. Our quote for this chapter is a classic instance of this. Smith has told us a lot about human nature already. In particular he's told us a lot about all the things the various parts of our nature make us want, from health and self-preservation to recognition and attention to tranquility and enjoyment to happiness and love. But just when you think he's finished discussing human nature and our natural desires, he adds one last point. Now he tells us that "man naturally desires" not just love (which we knew) but also "to be lovely." So just what does Smith think he's adding to the discussion here, and why exactly should we care?

We need to care about this, I think, because (at the risk of sounding hyperbolic) all of Smith's lessons on living a life from here on out depend on it. But that's of course a claim that you'll be able to judge only at the end of this book. For now, we simply need to be clear about what exactly Smith means by all of this. The key point is that as human beings we've been made in such a way that we want something more, when it comes to love, than simply getting love from others. Yes, we want to get love. But we also want to know that we really "deserve" the love we're trying to get—that we "deserve" to be loved even when nobody is actually giving us any love. This is what Smith means when he says that we naturally want to be "lovely." Today we generally use the word "lovely" (to the degree that we use it at all) to describe appearances. But Smith is using it to refer not to appearances, but to our moral worth. And when we put it this way we can see that he is making a big shift here. Up to now we've been discussing love as a good to be gotten. But in shifting from getting love to being lovely, Smith shifts from the sort of good that we get because we do a certain something to the sort of good that's ours because we are a certain something. This is an important shift of the question. No longer can we ask ourselves only: what must I do and how must I act in order to get the love that will make me happy? Now the question is rather: what must I be in order to be the sort of person who I know deserves and is worthy of love and praise?

Loveliness, that is, is a state of being: a state we occupy when we show ourselves "to be that thing which is the natural and proper object of love." And Smith extends this way of thinking to the related category of praise, explaining that "nature" has similarly "endowed" us "not only with a desire of being approved of, but with a desire of being what ought to be approved of."[1] This is crucial for several reasons, including its implications for social and political life.

Imagine a world in which all we cared about was being praised and loved and were indifferent to whether we actually deserved any of the praise or love we were chasing. In such a world we wouldn't bother caring about what kind of people we were. All our energy would go toward making sure we appeared a certain way to others, in the hopes that if we appear that certain way we might maximize our shot at getting the love and praise we seek. Now, I suspect that sort of world probably sounds awful to most readers of this book. That said, our own world—a world of selfies and image consultants and obsessive social media curation—may not be all that far removed from that world. In any case, it's clearly not the world Smith wants to encourage, nor the type of behavior he tends to admire; after all, it's only "the most frivolous and superficial of mankind," he tells us, who take pleasure in "that praise which they themselves know to be altogether unmerited."[2]

What most matters for us here isn't how our natural love of loveliness reshapes our social life, but how our natural love of loveliness necessarily shapes our very efforts to live our lives. And on this front, the key point is the difference between getting and deserving. When we're trying to get something, we're almost always trying to get something from a certain someone. Certainly that's true when we try to get attention or recognition or love (at least as we've been discussing love up to now). In these cases we act in accord with the side of our nature that is fundamentally needy and aims to satisfy its needs via exchange—the side of our nature that gives voice to the idea we met two chapters ago: "give me that which I want, and you shall have this which you want." But we do something else, and act from a different side of our nature, when we try to deserve something. In that case, we're not trying to get something, but are trying to be something, and specifically something that is worthy of measuring up to a certain standard.

Here's where the significance of this shift from getting to deserving lies. Deserved goods are different from gotten goods most of all in that gotten goods are not just given by others, but given by others who are the judges of whether or not we should get them at all. Admirers give attention because they think that the objects of their attention are worth it, perhaps because of their wealth or status or (hopefully) their merit. So too the objects of our beneficence love us because they think we've earned it by the love we've shown them. In these cases, it's the judgments of others that matter. But whose judgment matters when it comes to whether we're lovely or praiseworthy? That doesn't seem to be something that we can allow others to judge for us; in this case the only judge that matters is our own self—the only one who at the end of the day sees not just how we appear, but what we truly are. And if so, the goods we most need for happiness aren't the tributes of others but rather the tributes of our own consciences.

From this two specific questions emerge with regard to the challenge of living a life. First, in what exactly does worthiness consist? To use Smith's own words: what exactly is "that thing which is the natural and proper object of love"? Second, how are we to know if we ourselves are such a thing? How are we to judge whether we ourselves in fact deserve praise and love? The first is a question about how we define worthiness, the second one about how we judge worthiness: the first a question about what is deserving, the second a question about whether we are deserving. Both are questions we'll have to answer if we're serious about living life well. The greatest happiness depends on it: "what so great happiness as to be beloved, and to know that we deserve to be beloved?"[3]

XVII

———— ✶ ————

"When I endeavour to examine my own conduct, when I endeavour
to pass sentence upon it, and either to approve or condemn it,
it is evident that, in all such cases, I divide myself, as it were,
into two persons; and that I, the examiner and judge, represent
a different character from that other I, the person whose
conduct is examined into and judged of."

*Or: the path to healing our divisions begins with us first
further dividing ourselves.*

Last chapter left us with two questions. First, what is praiseworthiness? How can we define it? Second, how do we know
if we are praiseworthy? How should we judge it? Clearly we're
going to have to answer both questions if indeed "great happiness," as Smith told us, requires not just that we be loved by
others, but that we "know that we deserve to be loved." And in
the quote for this chapter, Smith takes a crucial step toward
providing his answer to the second question. How can we
judge whether we're praiseworthy in our own right? We first
need to divide ourselves into "two persons"—our regular person doing the acting and being observed and judged, and a second person, the "examiner and judge," who is in fact "a different character."

This turns out to be one of Smith's signature moves, and has been seen by many as the most important and original element of his moral philosophy: the "impartial spectator." In one short chapter, we can't hope to do justice to everything at stake with the concept of the impartial spectator. But we can, I think, try to get some clarity as to why the impartial spectator matters to those of us engaged in the project of trying to live a better life.

Let's begin with the problem of just why we need an impartial spectator in the first place. We know already that Smith thinks that genuine happiness requires that we not only are loved and praised, but also know that we deserve to be loved and praised. But who determines deservingness and worthiness? Other people can't do it for us; they know only what they see, and are often fooled by appearances. But we can't do it for ourselves either, at least in any simple sense. Sure, we know more of the full story of our inner thoughts and feelings and motives, the things that we often hide from others. But as human beings we tend not to be good judges in our own cases. We are of course creatures of self-interest, and our interest in thinking ourselves worthy is at odds with the objectivity and neutrality needed to guarantee the accuracy of judgments in matters that involve ourselves. Moreover, Smith also knows that we often willfully overlook certain aspects of ourselves that we don't like in order to focus on those things about ourselves that we do like. He calls this, memorably, the "mysterious veil of self-delusion," and insists that most of us find it hard (even painful) when we're presented with the whole truth about ourselves.[1]

In judgments of worth then we can't trust others and we can't trust ourselves. What to do? Smith's response is that we have to appeal to a different sort of person altogether, a sort of third person that lies between ourselves and others—one who is able to bring to its judgments the unique insights and perspectives of each party while being free of the biases characteristic of each party. When we do that, Smith says, we occupy the position of a "fair and impartial spectator," one able to judge worthiness free of all the potentially distorting effects of having a direct stake in the game.[2] And this is one way in which Smith's famous impartial spectator goes a bit beyond similar and more familiar principles like the Golden Rule. The Golden Rule tells us what to do and how to act in ways that are also intended to mitigate selfish behavior. But where the Golden Rule provides us with a guide for action, the impartial spectator is at least as concerned with teaching us how to judge—and how to judge moral merit in particular—as with teaching us how to act.

Smith's turn to the impartial spectator here has always struck me—and many others—as a brilliant solution to a very complex philosophical problem. Self-interest distorts our views on reality, but our imaginations provide us with the resources to create a new person who can correct our judgements in the real world. That again is an idea that deserves to be (and has been) studied carefully and thoroughly. But here I'll focus only on its implications for living a better life. And on this front two implications strike me as especially worthy of notice.

The first concerns what Smith is asking us to do in order to inhabit the perspective of the spectator. Look how he describes it in the quote for this chapter: if we want to pass judgment on our character and conduct, if we hope to be able to enter into the perspective of the impartial examiner and judge, we must first "divide" ourselves "into two persons." If you think through this a bit, you can see what a remarkable move is being made here. Our inquiry into the challenges of living a life began, after all, with the challenges of division. As Smith showed us at the beginning of this book, we are divided by nature (between self- and other-regarding feelings), and we are then further divided by our world (between our need for peace and tranquility and our world's incentivizing of fame and fortune). Division, that is, is the problem that our lives need to solve. But now it turns out that the path to healing our division begins with a self-conscious act of further division of our selves. In some very deep sense then, the achievement of the unity that is thwarted by our present division will require us not to resist division but to embrace it—albeit division of a particular sort, that is itself embraced in a particular way.

A second implication concerns what happens when we inhabit the perspective of an impartial observer of ourselves. Clearly, we learn a lot about ourselves—some of which we may like, some we might not like. But however cringe inducing the less likeable stuff may be, Smith thinks it's good for us to see it, as seeing it makes us more likely to make changes in the way we live. I once heard someone say the surest way to guarantee weight loss is to eat only when naked and in front of a mirror. That's not as poetic as how Smith puts it (and it's surely very bad diet advice), but Smith is after the same thing when he says, "if we saw ourselves in the light in which others see us," when it comes to our behavior "a reformation would generally be unavoidable" as "we could not otherwise endure the sight."[3]

But that's only part of what Smith has in mind when he talks about the reformation that inevitably follows when we see ourselves in a fair and impartial light. For it's not just that we change certain behaviors to bring them in line with our true self-interests: cutting back on desserts so that we can see washboard abs in the mirror. More importantly, seeing ourselves from this perspective reshapes how we relate to others. In fact, Smith tells us, "it is only by consulting this judge within, that we can ever see what relates to ourselves in its proper shape and dimensions; or that we can ever make any proper comparison between our own interests and those of other people."[4] And if that's right, then the act of becoming the impartial spectator of ourselves doesn't merely advance our promotion of our own self-betterment. It also fundamentally reshapes how we understand our own relationship to others. The division of ourselves into actor and spectator then isn't just an important step toward unity in ourselves, but also an important step in our efforts to achieve unity with others.

XVIII

———— ✳ ————

"When he views himself in the light in which he is conscious that
others will view him, he sees that to them he is but one of the
multitude in no respect better than any other in it."

Or: you aren't any better than anyone else—
and nobody else is any better than you.

The impartial spectator is quite a guy. For he—and he alone—
makes it possible for us to see ourselves as we really are. In particular, and as we saw at the very end of the last chapter, he allows us to "see what relates to ourselves in its proper shape and
dimensions." But what exactly does that mean? Exactly what
perspective on ourselves does he provide? As it turns out, it's
an extraordinary perspective, and one that most of us are
likely to find at least at first (and perhaps for a long time
after) very hard to swallow: that we are just "one of the multitude," in fact "in no respect better" than any other person in
that multitude.

This is quite a claim. Smith here tells us that if we do our job
well and fully inhabit the perspective of an impartial spectator
of ourselves, we'll come to realize that we have no claims to
thinking ourselves better than others. Now, in saying this,
Smith knows that he's asking a great deal of us. He himself,
after all, told us way back at the start of this book that we're

hardwired to think that our own selves and our own needs come first. He's also told us that our world rewards people of different status differently, showering recognition on the elite while overlooking the downtrodden. So Smith, maybe better than anyone, knows what he's up against in making this point—which is probably why he calls this the "hardest of all the lessons of morality."[1] Of course, the simple fact that a lesson is hard doesn't make it worthwhile. So why does Smith think that this particular lesson is so necessary for us to learn?

To help get our heads around this, I'd like to invoke the wisdom of my grandmother. She wasn't an academic, or even college educated, and I'm fairly sure she never read Adam Smith. But she understood as well as anyone what Smith is after here. She showed this in something she often said to her children, usually while wagging a finger: "Nobody is better than you, and you're not any better than anyone else!"

The first part of my grandmother's exhortation was surely shaped by the experience of living in an immigrant family in a new land in which there were no shortage of those who assumed their superiority to you. To believe, in that context, that nobody is better than you was to affirm the conviction of your inherent dignity, a dignity that transcends inequalities. That's a crucial service of this exhortation. But it's also the easier part of the exhortation to embrace. The harder part is the second part: acceptance that you're no better than anyone else. That's after all something very different from what we tend to tell our children today, especially when we tell them that they're special. Now, that's not wrong—I believe as much as I believe anything that every child is indeed special. At the same time, there's a world of difference between thinking that you're special and thinking that you're better than others, and I suspect this nuance is lost on most children who hear they're special (to say nothing of the adults these children in time become).

So why does all of this matter for those of us trying to figure out how best to live our lives? In the first place, Smith's hard lesson here teaches us a truth that's likely unpleasant at first but has the potential to be liberating. It's precisely that we're *not* special. Indeed, so far from being special, in all the things that really matter, it turns out that we're just another face in the crowd, no more special than anyone else. What's unpleasant about this thought is obvious: it's humbling. Indeed it's humbling almost to the same extent that telling a child that she is special is elevating. Now a child, at a certain stage in her development, may need to hear how special she is. But mature moral beings, Smith thinks, most need to hear and to embrace the opposite lesson—the lesson of the impartial spectator, delivered, as he says, in "a voice capable of astonishing the most presumptuous of our passions." We may not like it when it astonishes us in this way. But however unpleasant and astonishing this voice may be, it alone can enable us to overcome those "natural misrepresentations of self-love," and to embrace, instead, "the real littleness of ourselves, and of whatever relates to ourselves."[2]

Smith is asking us to do something here that's not just unpleasant, but difficult. The goal is for the individual to learn how to, as he says, "humble the arrogance of his self-love, and bring it down to something which other men can go along with."[3] What makes this so difficult for us is that this humbling goes against the natural grain of our self-love. And so it isn't enough for us merely to think certain thoughts or commit ourselves to certain kinds of principles in the abstract. Real self-control, Smith insists, requires more than "the abstruse syllogisms of a quibbling dialectic." Instead it demands our willingness to subject ourselves to a certain "discipline," and specifically the discipline of consciously conforming ourselves to the perspective of the impartial spectator.[4] If it wasn't clear before, it's surely clear now that Smith's philosophy isn't one of the seminar room, but one that regards life as a training ground on which we are continually being tested.

With that in place, let's turn from what's hard and painful here to what might make all this hard work and training worth it for us. I meant what I said when I said above that there's a sense in which the realization that we are just one of the multitude isn't just hard and humbling, but also liberating. The key point here is that the impartial spectator, even if he sometimes speaks in a voice that's hard for us to hear, enables us to see ourselves anew. Before becoming impartial spectators of ourselves, we tended to see the world through the lens of self-love. And seeing the world through this lens has two effects. First, when we see ourselves and our world through the lens of self-love we tend to magnify in importance all that concerns ourselves—often to the degree that we blow our concerns out of proportion. The result isn't just that we often make ourselves suffer a great deal of needless worry and anxiety. It also has a second implication. When self-love magnifies our self-concern it also crowds out others and their concerns from our vision. Wrapped up in ourselves and our lives because we think we matter so much, we render ourselves unable to see what matters to others. And it's from this confinement that the impartial spectator liberates us. When we embrace our "real littleness" we not only allow ourselves to let go of ourselves, but we also open ourselves up to others in a way that allows us to see what matters to them, and indeed, ultimately, why they themselves matter.

Finally (and maybe most importantly for the question at hand) when we embrace our real littleness we're also able to see more clearly what we're seeking when we set out to live our lives. Many people, as Smith has already had occasion to remark, live their lives in pursuit of greatness of some sort—greatness in wealth, greatness in power, greatness in status. But to believe in and to accept one's "real littleness" is to give up the idle pursuit of that sort of greatness forever. Our littleness isn't the kind of thing that can be remedied by greatness in those kinds of things. But what path of life, what sort of greatness, is suited to someone who at once accepts the truth of her littleness but yet wants to live the best life possible?

XIX

———— ★ ————

"The difference of natural talents in different men is,
in reality, much less than we are aware of."

*Or: however hard it may be for us to admit, nature made
us all more or less the same.*

In the quote for the previous chapter, Smith showed us how
the impartial spectator teaches us a hard but necessary lesson:
that we're equal to others, no better and no worse. In the quote
for this chapter, he goes a step further. For as it turns out, that
very hard and yet very necessary lesson of the impartial spectator is nothing more and nothing less than what nature had
always intended for us. Thus the point Smith wants to drive
home here: however much people may look different—and
however more talented some might seem, compared to others—
the truth is that these differences come "not so much from
nature, as from habit, custom, and education."

To make his point, Smith compares "a philosopher" to "a
common street porter." He chooses these figures because, he
thinks, to most people they look like the "most dissimilar
characters." Whenever I read this passage I think of my father.
My father knew something about both the blue-collar and
white-collar worlds, and he liked to say you could know a lot
about a man from the condition of his hands. It's the sort of

observation Smith draws on here. He knows we often classify and rank people by their appearances and their jobs. But Smith's aim here isn't to pass judgment on this. What he's focused on here is to make sure instead that these sorts of habitual judgments don't blind us to the truth that many people—especially those at the top—often don't want to admit. The truth, as Smith puts it, is that at birth, and even "for the first six or eight years" of their lives, the future philosopher and the future porter were so similar that "neither their parents nor play-fellows could perceive any remarkable difference." Only as the effects of "habit, custom, and education" began to kick in did they start seeming different. And in time, Smith explains, habit and custom and education caused this difference to reach the point where "the vanity of the philosopher" causes him "to acknowledge scarce any resemblance" between himself and the porter.[1]

This is a very charged claim. Why did it matter so much to Smith? And why might it matter for us? I think it matters for a few reasons. First, it shows that Smith wasn't above self-criticism. At different places in his work Smith criticizes certain types of businessmen and certain types of politicians. But for all this he didn't let his own profession off the hook. Far from it: with all the world's professions to choose from, when it came time to choose an example of someone whose vanity leads him to think he's better than others, the onetime Professor of Moral Philosophy at the University of Glasgow chose a philosopher. I have to say that I admire this: both for what it says about Smith, and for how it captures so well the characteristic vice of us academics. Max Weber much later would famously call vanity the "occupational disease" of scholars, but this is something that Smith knew long before.[2]

But Weber isn't the only one in the history of philosophy to write about this idea. And sometimes I wonder whether Smith might not have had in mind some of these other accounts. For example, in a famous moment in Plato's *Republic*, Socrates explains that in the ideal city, the people will need to be taught what he calls a "noble lie." There are actually several parts to this noble lie, but the part relevant for us is where Socrates says that the citizens of the ideal city should be brought up to believe that they were born with a certain metal in their soul, and that those born with gold in their souls have been made by nature to be better than those born with souls of iron.[3] Now, what Socrates very pointedly labels a lie, lots of philosophers (and others) in his wake have taken as a self-aggrandizing truth, one that justifies the idea that some people are somehow naturally superior to other people. But Smith clearly pushes back against all of this, insisting that human beings are in fact naturally equal as far as their talents and abilities go.

Smith's claim about the natural equality of human beings thus distances him from Plato and Socrates. But it also brings him closer to our world. The quote on which we've been focusing in this chapter is the second of two quotes in this book from the *Wealth of Nations*. Coming as it does in Smith's book of 1776, this quote brings to my mind at least another document of the same year that also had something remarkable to say about the natural equality of human beings. When Thomas Jefferson and the other drafters of the Declaration of Independence proclaimed it to be "self-evident, that all men are created equal," they took a stand in line with Smith's. For Smith and the Founders agree that there exist certain natural equalities among human beings that mark us as deserving of decent and dignified treatment and also render illegitimate certain types of human behavior.

At the same time there's a subtle but important difference between Jefferson's claim and Smith's claim here. The Declaration suggests that the equality of human beings is most evident in the fact that all human beings have been "endowed by their Creator with certain unalienable rights." But Smith suggests that the equality of human beings is evident in the fact that we have all been given roughly equal "natural talents." Talents are different from rights, of course. And focusing on talents—and specifically focusing on the question of the ways in which human beings born with equal natural talents have become so different in the course of their development—may lead those of us interested in the question of living well to ask how we came to be what we are. Those who have been particularly fortunate in their lives may especially be led to wonder who deserves the credit for their successes. Do our parents deserve it for the genes they gave us? Do we ourselves deserve it for the hard work that enabled us to advance? Do our teachers deserve it for the effort they put into our education and cultivation? Or, in the end, is it just sheer luck of the draw: the lottery of life that placed some of us in a position where we had more chances to flourish than those born into other positions?

It feels good to tell ourselves that we earned our successes through our own efforts. But Smith, in emphasizing the outsized role of "custom, habit, and education" in this, gives us some reason to think that the successful aren't quite as much the masters of their fate as they sometimes think. Reflecting on this may even lead the fortunate to see themselves a little more humbly and the less fortunate a little more generously. And in this respect this sort of reflection may be of great help to the impartial spectator's efforts to teach us that "hardest of all the lessons of morality."

XX

"To deserve, to acquire, and to enjoy the respect and admiration
of mankind, are the great objects of ambition and emulation.
Two different roads are presented to us, equally leading to
the attainment of this so much desired object; the one, by the
study of wisdom and the practice of virtue; the other,
by the acquisition of wealth and greatness."

*Or: we need to choose between the road admired by the world
and the road less traveled.*

It's time for us to start making some choices. Smith has made a
number of claims so far about who we are and what we naturally need and want. He's also shown us quite a bit about our
world, and what it tends to reward. But in light of all this, and
especially in light of the fact that the clocks of our lives are
continuing to tick, we need to get about making our decision
and pursuing one path of life or another.

In this lovely passage Smith lays out as clearly as he can the
essential choice that we have to make. In so doing, he takes the
liberty of reducing our choice down to two options. In fact, if
you look at the paragraph in which the quote from this chapter is to be found, you can see how intent Smith is on putting
these two options before us. The whole paragraph is itself set
up around this binary, insisting that in the end there are only

"two different roads" and "two different characters" and "two different models" and "two different pictures" that we have to choose between.[1] So what are they, and which for us is it going to be?

The second road is the more traveled. It's the road followed by "the rich and the great," those ambitious for the rewards that the world has to offer. Smith, it has to be said, doesn't paint this world in the most attractive colors. This, after all, is a world "of proud ambition and ostentatious avidity," populated by the sort of characters who are "gaudy and glittering" in their appearance.[2] By now, we know the type—both from what Smith has told us, and from just living in the world and keeping our eyes open. These are the people who are full of themselves—people who, maybe even because they're full of themselves, tend to be the ones in positions of authority. We see this especially in politics: a world in which, as Smith says, an election winner is often just "some impudent blockhead who entertains no doubt about his own qualifications."[3] But I'm not eager to take cheap shots at politicians here. The key point is that this same self-aggrandizement that often strikes us as so vulgar and so off-putting is often precisely what enables its possessors to be successful. Smith is clear on this: "great success in the world, great authority over the sentiments and opinions of mankind, have very seldom been acquired without some degree of this excessive self-admiration." For in the end it's precisely this "excessive presumption" that "dazzles the multitude, and often imposes even upon those who are much superior to the multitude."[4]

For anyone trying to make sense of politics today, there's a lot of food for thought here. But what does all of this mean for our concerns regarding living a life? For that we have to look at the other road Smith describes: the road not of wealth and greatness, but of "the study of wisdom and the practice of virtue." Whatever else it may be, this is the direct opposite of the road taken by those ambitious for wealth and greatness. Where that road was one of pride and ostentatiousness, this is one of "humble modesty and equitable justice." Where that was gaudy and glittering, this is "more correct and more exquisitely beautiful." Maybe most importantly, where the travelers of that road force themselves "upon the notice of every wandering eye," those who choose to follow this road are likely to find themselves "attracting the attention of scarce any body but the most studious and careful observer." For in the end, Smith would have us know, it is only "a small party, who are the real and steady admirers of wisdom and virtue"—a party dwarfed by that "great mob of mankind" who are the "admirers and worshippers" of wealth and greatness.

So this second road is clearly the road less traveled.[5] But what reason is there to believe that the less traveled road is really the better road? A few points deserve mention on this front, some of which hearken back to themes raised in earlier chapters. First, back in chapter 8 we saw how necessary tranquility is for happiness. If that's so, the second road, in its obscurity, seems more likely to lead to tranquility than the first road with all its gaudy grandeur and obsession with public appearance. Second, back in chapter 13 we saw how necessary love is for happiness. If that's so, the second road, dedicated as it is to the practice of virtue, seems more likely to earn us the love of others than the first road in its focus on self-love. But most importantly, and put in the terms of the conclusion that ended chapter 18, that first and better traveled road is suited to those who seek greatness as it's conventionally understood. But it's not a road available to those who have become, thanks to the impartial spectator, convinced of their "real littleness." For them (I want to say "for us"), once convinced that we're in fact just one of the multitude, the greatness that we seek can't be measured by comparing ourselves and our attainments to others. That's of course what those competitors for wealth and recognition have dedicated their lives to. But travelers on the other road need another very different standard by which to measure their progress—itself a point to which we will return later.

For now though, let's assume that Smith is right, and that we'll be more likely to get the goods most necessary for happiness if we follow the less traveled road, the road of "the study of wisdom and the practice of virtue." This leaves us with at least two questions that we'll need to answer. First, what in the world is "wisdom," and where exactly do we find it? Second, what exactly is "virtue," and why is it so important to us if we want to live our lives as well as possible?

XXI

———— ✳ ————

"The man of the most perfect virtue, the man whom we naturally
love and revere the most, is he who joins, to the most perfect
command of his own original and selfish feelings, the most exquisite
sensibility both to the original and sympathetic feelings of others."

Or: perfect virtue requires that we develop two different types of virtues.

The road more traveled is that of wealth and greatness. The
road less traveled is that of wisdom and virtue. But what exactly does it mean to be wise and virtuous? Smith gets us
started on this question here by describing "the man of the
most perfect virtue." It is here that he begins to define what
virtue is. But he's of course doing so in an interesting way. Most
of us, when we define terms and concepts, try to explain them.
But Smith is here focused less on explaining than on showing;
he defines virtue by sketching us a portrait of a particular type
of person. So who is this "man of the most perfect virtue," and
what exactly makes him so special?

The first thing to note is that this is a person not just of
ordinary goodness, but of "the most perfect virtue." Smith, as
it turns out, isn't shy when it comes to using the word "perfect." This makes him different from most moral philosophers today, who tend not to be quite as comfortable with
talk of perfection. That's the language of ancient philosophy,

which conceived of the human being as having a specific purpose. On that view, perfection lies in achieving or fulfilling our natural end goal. Smith isn't a teleological thinker in quite this sense, for even if he does think that we're "made for" something (as we saw back in the third chapter), he doesn't think that there's simply one specific way that all human beings have to go about doing what we're made to do if we're to achieve perfect virtue. But more important for now is the fact that here and elsewhere, Smith embraces the language of the perfect. So this compels us to ask: just what does it mean to speak of perfection if we don't also buy into teleology? How are we to measure perfection if we don't have access to some vision of the natural end or purpose of a human being? I don't think that this is a question we can answer quite yet, but it's an important question and we need to have it on the table.

A second and related point also worth noting concerns Smith's use of the language of virtue. Virtue is another concept that we tend to associate more with the ancient moral philosophers than modern moral philosophers. It would be wrong to suggest that modern philosophers have given up on virtue; the resurgence of what has come to be known as "virtue ethics" is enough to put the lie to that.[1] At the same time, when ethicists speak of virtue today, some often have in mind something more like life skills or character strengths rather than the sort of all-encompassing excellence on which ancient studies of virtue like Plato's *Meno* or Aristotle's *Nicomachean Ethics* focused. But this is another place where it may be that Smith is more ancient than modern. In his view, virtue isn't simply a skill or a strength. It's more than that. "Virtue is excellence," Smith tells us, "something uncommonly great and beautiful, which rises far above what is vulgar and ordinary."[2] This too isn't how modern philosophers tend to talk, and indeed in invoking these categories of beautiful and transcendent excellence, Smith again speaks an ancient language.

But all of this is still prefatory to the main issue at hand. It's all well and good to say that a person of perfect virtue has some sort of lofty excellence. But what is it exactly about this person that distinguishes her as lofty? Is there something specific that she is or does—something that we in our own right can be or do if we hope to participate in an excellence of this sort? To this end, Smith outlines two specific attributes of this person. In so doing he shifts the question slightly—away from the abstract category of "virtue" in the singular to the more concrete category of "virtues" in the plural.

On this front, Smith's key point is that a person of the most perfect virtue is defined by her possession of what he elsewhere calls "two different sets of virtues."[3] And in the sentence that immediately follows the quote for this chapter he makes clear exactly what these two sets of virtues are. Here he says that the person who "must surely be the natural and proper object of our highest love and admiration" is the person who "to all the soft, the amiable, and the gentle virtues, joins all the great, the awful, and the respectable." Smith's aim here is to divide the virtues into two classes. On one hand are the virtues that concern our relationship with ourselves. Their purpose is to diminish our sensitivity to ourselves, and thereby help us get a command and control over our "selfish feelings." These he calls the "awful virtues"—awful in the sense that they require us to exercise an uncompromising harsh discipline over ourselves. On the other hand are the virtues that concern the ways in which we relate to others. Just as the awful virtues decrease our sensitivity to ourselves, the second sort of virtues aim to increase our sensitivity to others, and are "amiable" insofar as they encourage "sympathetic feelings."[4]

It's easy enough to understand how Smith has divided the virtues up. But why does he divide them up into precisely these categories? The back story concerns his vision of the dynamic between actors and spectators that defines moral life and moral decision making. We are, Smith thinks, constantly engaged in exchanges of sympathy with those around us; when we act a certain way, we anticipate that those who see us act this way will (or won't) "enter into" our perspective and sympathize with us. And of course we want this sympathy given the way we're made. So what these two classes of virtues do is maximize the chances that we'll get the sympathy we desire by bringing us more in line with how spectators of our behavior actually feel when they see us. When we exercise the awful virtues to lower the pitch of our selfish feelings, we more closely approximate the feelings that impartial spectators of our behavior are likely to feel when they see us. When we exercise the amiable virtues to ramp up the feelings we feel for others, we raise ourselves up to a level closer to what others feel for themselves. Thus Smith's claim that "upon these two different efforts, upon that of the spectator to enter into the sentiments of the person principally concerned, and upon that of the person principally concerned, to bring down his emotions to what the spectator can go along with, are founded two different sets of virtues."[5]

But all of this merely explains how Smith's theory of the virtues fits into his broader system. Why exactly does it matter for those of us mainly concerned with living a better life? To see this we need to see just what Smith is asking of us here. Smith's is a quite unique view of human excellence. Many are the thinkers out there who privilege one type of virtue over another. Tough types tend to like the awful virtues; they admire those who declare victory over themselves—those who are able, thanks to toughness and grit, to sit with the pain and discomfort that come from suffering and unfulfilled desire. More tender types tend to like the amiable virtues; they admire gentle and compassionate souls able to feel the pains felt by others. But Smith's vision of virtue aims to combine these, in the belief that as different as these different virtues may be, in the end you can't have one without the other, if indeed you aspire to be the kind of person "we naturally love and revere the most."

XXII

———— ✳ ————

"Hence it is, that to feel much for others and little for ourselves, that
to restrain our selfish, and to indulge our benevolent affections,
constitutes the perfection of human nature; and can alone
produce among mankind that harmony of sentiments and
passions in which consists their whole grace and propriety."

Or: our individual perfection is not only good for ourselves;
it's also good for society.

With these words, Smith reprises the lesson of the chapter
before—but with a twist. Here, in showing us what "the perfection of human nature" looks like, he reiterates what he
showed us in his portrait of the "man of the most perfect virtue." For here again, the mark of perfection is minimization of
selfishness and maximization of benevolence; the amiable and
awful virtues of the previous chapter are reprised in Smith's insistence that if we hope to achieve perfection, we need to strive
to "feel much for others and little for ourselves."[1]

All that we knew already. But what this account adds to the
previous one is a new account of why exactly perfection of this
sort is good. To see this we have to call again to mind the standards we've been using in discussing goodness throughout this
inquiry. In terms of the challenge of living a life, goodness, as
we've seen, has two components: good to self and good to

others. So exactly how is this "perfection of human nature" good in both of these ways? In the previous chapter we saw that being perfect in the way Smith describes perfection is good for us insofar as it renders us "the natural and proper object" of the love and admiration of others. Smith again means by this that a person of perfect virtue, even if he or she doesn't always receive the love and admiration of others, is yet the person who is most worthy and deserving of their love and admiration. And as we've seen, it's worthiness that we most desire, and on which our real happiness depends.

But self-perfection isn't just good for us ourselves: it's also good for others. This is the crucial twist that Smith here adds to what we've already seen. On this front, his main point is that when we perfect our natures by adopting the virtues that enable us to feel so much for others and so little for ourselves, we also promote the perfection of society. This comes out in the claim that this particular type of individual perfection produces in society a "harmony of sentiments and passions." Moreover Smith insists not only that perfection of this sort fosters harmony among mankind, but that it "alone" can produce this harmony. In any case, the key point here is that it's not just the individual who benefits from the pursuit of self-perfection, but "mankind."

This is a striking claim, and we need to pause on it for a moment. In part it's striking for its insistence that self-perfection and the perfection of mankind go hand in hand; Smith upends a lot of zero-sum and either-or thinking in suggesting this. But what's most striking here is Smith's suggestion that social living at its best is defined by a condition of "harmony of sentiments." That's very different from how we, the direct heirs of his liberal vision, tend to understand the good society. We say that the good society is the one in which freedom is maximized, or in which equality is guaranteed, or in which justice is secured. And we who value these ideals often profess ourselves willing to fight for them, even if it means pushing back on a popular consensus and making waves. But Smith is opening up a very different vision of social perfection here, one that moves in a different direction than at least some of what we have grown accustomed to believe. As such, we'll have to decide for ourselves how far we want to follow him in prizing the "harmony" of mankind and indeed the "grace" that is made possible by this harmony. But living as we do in a moment when our society is more divided and more split and less harmonious than it has been for some time, now might be a good time to ask if there might not be something in Smith's vision of a society of harmony and grace that can usefully supplement, if not supplant, the society dedicated to agonistic claims of rights and recognition.

However this may be, Smith has taken a crucial step here toward providing us with useful guidance on our key question. We've been seeking a single life that is both good for us and good for others, and in his accounts of the person of perfect virtue and also of the perfection of human nature, he has sought to provide us with a vision of such a life. At the same time, some of us might be troubled by a lingering question. All this talk of perfection—what exactly justifies it? We know already that Smith isn't quite talking about perfection in the same way as the ancients did. So how exactly is he using the term? And maybe even more importantly, does Smith really think that perfection is something human beings can actually achieve?

Smith addresses these questions when he describes, in two different places in *The Theory of Moral Sentiments*, what exactly "perfection" is. Perfection, he explains, can be taken in two different senses, employing "two different standards." The first concerns the idea of "absolute perfection" or "complete propriety and perfection." And this, he says, is a perfection that "no human conduct ever did, or ever can come up to." But the second sense of perfection concerns "that degree of proximity or distance from this complete perfection, which the actions of the greater part of men commonly arrive at"—"the common degree of excellence which is usually attained" in various human endeavors.[2] Now, several things are worth noting about this account of perfection. First, Smith doesn't think that "absolute perfection" is humanly attainable. So when he talks about that person "of the most perfect virtue" or about the "perfection of human nature," insofar as he's talking specifically about *human* virtue he can't be talking about perfection in the first or absolute sense, but only in the second: the sort of perfection that is actually attainable by human beings. Second, even though Smith thinks it is not possible for us to become perfect in that first sense, we yet need to make sure that we never lose sight of this first type of perfection, and limit our vision to the second type only. To see why, we need to turn to his portrait of the one who most fully succeeds at the project of living a life: the one who, as he says, carries human nature up to "the highest degree of perfection," who represents "the utmost perfection of all the intellectual and of all the moral virtues"—the one who, most importantly, embodies "the most perfect wisdom combined with the most perfect virtue."[3]

XXIII

———— ✳ ————

"The wise and virtuous man directs his principal attention to the
first standard; the idea of exact propriety and perfection."

*Or: the wisdom of the wise and virtuous lies in
their vision of perfection.*

It's time now for the main event. Smith has been describing, in
various ways, the sorts of things that a good life requires us to
think and to do and to be. But now the time has come for him
to show us exactly what this life looks like. He does so in the
portrait he paints of the one he calls "the wise and virtuous
man."[1] This wise and virtuous man is in a real sense the peak
figure of his ethics, the person whom we readers are being
challenged to emulate in our own ways, in our lives. But what
exactly makes this person so special?

The wise and virtuous man's very name is a clue as to what
makes him so admirable. The wise and virtuous person is distinguished by possessing both wisdom and virtue. And that's
an accomplishment in itself. Ancient philosophers like Plato
and Aristotle often distinguished the life of wisdom embodied
by philosophers from the lives of ethical virtue embodied by
good citizens and gentlemen. Thinkers up to our own day have
continued to make much of this distinction, emphasizing the
difference between the *vita completiva* and the *vita activa*.[2] But

Smith rejects this division. For him, true excellence lies not in choosing between but in combining these two types of excellence. The wise and virtuous person is precisely the one whose virtue informs her wisdom, and whose wisdom informs her virtue.

At the same time we can't see how exactly wisdom and virtue work together until we have a sense of what exactly wisdom and virtue are unto themselves. In this chapter I try to tackle the idea of this peak figure's wisdom, and in the next chapter I'll try to tackle the idea of this peak figure's virtue, and how it is informed by this wisdom. But it's enough just to try to define wisdom, so let's let that be our task for the rest of this chapter.

So in what exactly does the wise and virtuous person's wisdom consist? The quote for this chapter suggests that it lies in such a person's single-minded attention to a concept that we've met already: namely the idea of what Smith earlier called "absolute perfection." We remember that Smith thinks there are two kinds of perfection: the absolute perfection that no human activity can ever attain, and the relative perfection that distinguishes the best of actual human activities. The wise and virtuous man is aware of the second standard, but it isn't what occupies his "principal attention." Instead it's the "first standard" that he sets his sights on.

This raises several questions. First, how exactly does such a person come to know just what this absolute or "exact propriety and perfection" looks like? After all, Smith has gone out of his way to tell us that this is a level that no human conduct has ever quite lived up to. So where exactly did the wise and virtuous man get this lofty idea that he organizes his life around? Smith's response is remarkable. It's all the more remarkable when we see how it differs from other accounts of where we get the idea of perfection from. Think back again to ancient philosophy. Plato, for example, famously taught that there were, in a realm above us, "forms" that represent perfections of various types, and that required a sort of divine illumination or philosophical genius for us to see. Christianity has a different idea of perfection to be sure, but it too teaches that if we hope to see perfection we need revelation, a gift of grace bringing sight to the blind and enabling us to bear witness to a perfection transcending the things of this world. But Smith's wise and virtuous man takes a different route. The perfection he sees isn't one that is in some sense "out there," requiring a special revelation to see, but one that is in fact very much a thing of our world "down here"—and indeed in two senses.

First, far from insisting that the idea of this lofty perfection is given to only a few, Smith says that in fact "there exists in the mind of every man, an idea of this kind." What makes the wise and virtuous person unique then isn't the simple fact that he has this idea—after all, it's in "every man"—but the work he's put into developing this idea.

This leads to a second sense in which his idea of perfection is a thing of the world "down here." His idea of perfection, so far from being attained by transcending this world, is the result of his careful observation of and induction from the things of this world. Smith indeed conspicuously emphasizes throughout this account the crucial role of spectatorship and observation. The wise and virtuous man's idea of perfection, he explains, is "gradually formed from his observations upon the conduct both of himself and of other people." It takes "slow, gradual, and progressive work" over the course of time to develop: "every day some feature is improved; every day some blemish is corrected." The key point here is that this process begins with observations that "have been made with the most acute and delicate sensibility" and "the utmost care and attention." It's this careful observation and assiduous study, not revelation or philosophical genius, that enables such a person to have "formed a much more correct image" of perfection, and indeed to be "much more deeply enamoured of its exquisite and divine beauty" than are other people.[3]

The perfection to which the wise and virtuous person directs her attention is then an idea that has been generated, as it were, from the bottom up, rather than given from on high. But even if this explains how and from where the wise person gets this idea, it doesn't explain why this idea matters for how a wise and virtuous person (or someone who aspires to become wise and virtuous) lives her life. And Smith clearly thinks that wisdom of this sort matters quite a bit, since it changes our life, and indeed changes it forever. In fact, this sort of wisdom, so far from excusing its possessors from virtue and allowing them to retreat into the quiet worlds of theory or philosophy, is precisely what enables them and indeed compels them to live lives of active virtue. Wisdom does this by fundamentally reshaping their relationships—their relationships both to others and to their own selves.

XXIV

———— ✳ ————

"His whole mind, in short, is deeply impressed, his whole behaviour
and deportment are distinctly stamped with the character of real
modesty; with that of a very moderate estimation of his own merit,
and, at the same time, of a full sense of the merit of other people."

*Or: the virtue of the wise and virtuous lies in
their humility and beneficence.*

We know already that wise and virtuous people are wise, and
that their wisdom is to be found in their appreciation of perfection. But how exactly are they virtuous, and what if anything does their virtue have to do with their wisdom? In developing his account of the wise and virtuous person Smith
answers these questions, showing us not only that wisdom of
the sort he's described decisively shapes virtue, but that it
shapes it in two ways—first by reshaping our relationship to
ourselves, and second by reshaping our relationships to others.

Let's start with the first category, the wise and virtuous
man's relationship to his own self. As we've seen, the wisdom
of such a person enables him to generate a vision of absolute
perfection from his observations of and reflections on ordinary life. This is quite an accomplishment unto itself. But it's
what such a person does with this vision that makes him not
only wise but virtuous. Put simply, a wise and virtuous person

knows his work isn't done once he's developed a vision of perfection. Of course, you could hardly blame him if he did. If at that point all he wanted was to be left alone to bask in the beauty of what he'd seen, many of us would probably say he's earned it. Through remarkable effort he's enabled himself to see something very few will ever see so clearly. And imagine what the rest of the world must look like to one who has seen the sort of perfection he's seen. In comparison, everything else must look ugly and repulsive, just as it does to the one liberated from the cave in Plato's famous allegory.[1] Wouldn't you, if you were such a person, want to stay in the world of the perfect and beautiful rather than be compelled to come back to the world of the imperfect and ugly?

But in fact it's precisely this that the wise and virtuous man does. So far from sitting forever with his vision of absolute perfection, the wise and virtuous man takes the vision of absolute perfection that his wisdom has afforded him and carries it with him back into the real world, using it as a standard with which to judge the things of this world. And what is even more remarkable is that, among the things of this world that he judges in this way, the one on which he focuses most of all is himself. A wise and virtuous man strives to become an impartial spectator of himself, and is most concerned to apply the standard of absolute perfection so that he can see how he measures up.

This turns out to be a painful undertaking. It may even be more painful than the arduous process of generating this vision of perfection in the first place. For when we take absolute perfection as the yardstick to measure ourselves against, Smith thinks even "the wisest and best of us all, can, in his own character and conduct, see nothing but weakness and imperfection; can discover no ground for arrogance and presumption, but a great deal for humility, regret, and repentance." Yet it's a task that the wise and virtuous man doesn't shy away from. He knows that he's pretty good at what he does, and that if he were content to compare himself to others, he'd have reason to be proud. But having caught a glimpse of genuine perfection, the whole project of comparing himself to others no longer seems very interesting or important. At that point there's neither much pleasure nor much pride to be taken in comparisons of that sort, which is why Smith says such a person is "necessarily much more humbled by the one comparison, than he ever can be elevated by the other."[2]

So one consequence of a wise and virtuous man's wisdom is that this wisdom serves to teach him "real modesty" and "humility." Having seen perfection, afterward he always "remembers, with concern and humiliation" how frequently he "has so far departed from that model." Wisdom thus leads to virtue by precluding pride and restraining egocentrism. In this sense the wise and virtuous person's wisdom complements and completes the work of both the impartial spectator and the awful virtues. But the wisdom of such a person also shapes her relationship to others.

Thus the second way wisdom complements virtue. Smith develops his argument on this front by showing us just how the wise and virtuous person's vision of perfection leads her to rethink not just her own imperfection but also the imperfections of others. Noting that a wise and virtuous man "is never so elated as to look down with insolence even upon those who are really below him," Smith tells us that he

feels so well his own imperfection, he knows so well the difficulty with which he attained his own distant approximation to rectitude, that he cannot regard with contempt the still greater imperfection of other people. Far from insulting over their inferiority, he views it with the most indulgent commiseration, and, by his advice as well as example, is at all times willing to promote their further advancement.[3]

Ultimately then, a wise and virtuous man isn't contemptuous of that most basic concern of human beings to better their condition. It's true that he's indifferent to his own condition, and doesn't give much thought to trying to raise himself above others in wealth or status or power. Bettering the condition of others—striving at all times "to promote their further advancement"—is however the project of a wise and virtuous person's life.

What ultimately makes the wise and virtuous man special and unique then is his conscious privileging of the interests of actual others as well as the interest of society above his own interests. Smith is explicit about this: "the wise and virtuous man," he tells us, "is at all times willing that his own private interest should be sacrificed to the public interest of his own particular order or society."[4] In so doing, he again bears witness to the degree to which he takes to heart the voice and lessons of the impartial spectator, who teaches him that he is not only "but one of the multitude" and "of no more consequence than any other in it," but also "bound at all times to sacrifice and devote himself to the safety, to the service, and even to the glory of the greater number."[5]

And with this, it's clear just why Smith thinks this life is good for others. The wise and virtuous person, in serving others and in always striving for their well-being, lives a life that is good for those who live with her, a point that hardly needs elaborating. But the way that Smith has made his point makes it much less easy to see how exactly the life of the wise and virtuous person can be good for the wise and virtuous person herself. After all, Smith has just asked this person explicitly to "sacrifice" herself for others—to sacrifice the pleasure of contemplating perfection for a life of active service, to sacrifice promoting her own self-interest in order to promote the interests of others. So even if it's clear what others gain from having this sort of person around, just what is it that makes it all worth it for someone who lives this life?

XXV

---- ✳ ----

"Though a wise man feels little pleasure from praise where he knows
there is no praise-worthiness, he often feels the highest in doing
what he knows to be praise-worthy, though he knows equally well
that no praise is ever to be bestowed upon it."

*Or: the reward of the wise and virtuous person is the
pleasure of self-approbation.*

The goal of our inquiry has been to identify the life that is at
once both good for self and good for others. Smith, in his inquiry, identifies the life of the wise and virtuous man as the
best life. How that life is good for others is clear: the wise and
virtuous man dedicates his life to bettering the condition of
others. But just how is such a life good for the one who lives it?
How could it really be in anyone's interest to live such a life if
living it requires the "sacrifice" of "private interest"? Here
Smith gives his answer: not only do we get "pleasure" from knowing that we're praiseworthy, but in fact we get the "highest"
pleasure.

Thus Smith's paradox: by sacrificing our interests we realize
a deeper self-interest. Or put differently: only by forgoing familiar pleasures and doing painful work do we come in time to
experience the highest pleasures. The pleasures and interests
sacrificed here of course are the familiar pleasures of attention

and recognition and praise that we know are a driving force in so many lives. These aren't concerns worthy of a truly wise person: "to show much anxiety about praise, even for praiseworthy actions, is seldom a mark of great wisdom, but generally of some degree of weakness."[1] It isn't then the esteem of others or a desire for rewards and recognition that leads an individual who is genuinely dedicated to wisdom and virtue to live as she does. And Smith is explicit about this, insisting in our quote for this chapter that the wise and virtuous person's resolve to act as she does isn't diminished even by knowing that "no praise is ever to be bestowed on it." Indeed "the character of the most exalted wisdom and virtue" lies specifically in never allowing our benevolent temper "to be damped or discouraged by the malignity and ingratitude of the individuals towards whom it may have been exercised."[2]

At the end of chapter 14 we wondered if there can be a place in Smith for love without hope of recompense. And now we see that there is: the wise and virtuous person works without hope of reward and loves knowing she won't be loved in return. But why? What is it that keeps someone going down this path of life—always working for others, never promoting herself, all the while knowing that nobody is ever going to recognize her for all this? Smith's answer is that such people do what they do because they care more for their own approval than for the approval of others. "Self-approbation," that is, "if not the only, is at least the principal object" with which a wise and virtuous person is concerned, for indeed "the love of it, is the love of virtue."[3] And, when you think about it, this makes sense. Someone who has dedicated his whole life to trying to understand perfection isn't likely to take much pleasure in the praises of people who haven't thought about perfection. Nor is he likely to be much troubled by the criticism of these sorts of people, even when directed to him. This is why Smith says "we can be more indifferent about the applause, and, in some measure, despise the censure of the world" if our self-approbation renders us "secure that, however misunderstood and misrepresented, we are the natural and proper objects of approbation."[4]

The life of wisdom and virtue is likely to strike some people as a missed opportunity—a life of interests forsaken and pleasures renounced. But that's only because many people are capable of judging only by appearances. If we were able to see into wise and virtuous people, Smith thinks we'd see that their lives provide them with not only the pleasure and the consciousness of praiseworthiness but even the tranquility and freedom from anxiety that all of us, Smith thinks, are seeking. "Misery and wretchedness can never enter the breast in which dwells complete self-satisfaction," he tells us.[5] In the end then, what makes the wise and virtuous person's life worth it is that it succeeds in gratifying the deepest interests of the best sort of human being. Indeed to live like this is to live at the very edge of human potential:

> The man who acts solely from a regard to what is right and fit to be done, from a regard to what is the proper object of esteem and approbation, though these sentiments should never be bestowed upon him, acts from the most sublime and godlike motive which human nature is even capable of conceiving.[6]

XXVI

———— ✦ ————

"The most sublime speculation of the contemplative philosopher
can scarce compensate the neglect of the smallest active duty."

Or: it's not enough to be wise if one hopes to be wise and virtuous.

When Smith speaks of "the most sublime and godlike motive
which human nature is even capable of conceiving," as he did
in the conclusion to the previous chapter, he speaks a striking
language. Most of us today don't tend to talk about human
beings, even when they are at their very best, as "sublime and
godlike." We talk about good people and good deeds, but
"sublime and godlike" suggests an altogether different way of
thinking about goodness, one that opens up a horizon that
transcends the more ordinary sort of goodness that we're used
to seeing and describing here on earth.

To find people talking this sort of language, the language of
transcendence, we need to look beyond philosophy as we usually understand it today. Talk of transcendence tends to make
many philosophers today uncomfortable. That's the language
of religion, and, to some degree, the language of certain pre-
modern and non-Western philosophies. Yet Smith, interestingly, doesn't seem to have any problem using this language
when it comes to describing the peak figure of his ethics, the
wise and virtuous person. And this prompts several questions,

not least of which is how exactly Smith's wise and virtuous person compares to other peak figures who likewise have been regarded as transcending the ordinary boundaries of human excellence.

Two specific figures come to mind on this front. They are the same two that Smith's friend Benjamin Franklin famously invoked in his own remarkable account of his methods for succeeding at "the bold and arduous project of arriving at moral perfection." Franklin, to this end, notoriously generated a list of thirteen virtues. The last of these was "humility," to which he annexed the precept "imitate Jesus and Socrates."[1] Of all that can and should be said about Franklin's exhortation, I'll restrict myself to one question for now. Namely: how does Smith's transcendent paragon of excellence, the wise and virtuous man, compare to Jesus and Socrates, the Western tradition's classic models of the life of transcendent excellence?

Let's start with Socrates. Socrates has long served as the key point of reference for self-conscious attempts at self-fashioning by thinking individuals concerned to live the best life possible.[2] And Socrates in fact figures prominently (or at least not infrequently) in *The Theory of Moral Sentiments*. For the most part Smith takes Socrates to represent an excellence commensurate with that of the wise and virtuous man. And this is evident most of all to Smith in Socrates' attitude toward death.

Death turns out to be a prominent theme in *The Theory of Moral Sentiments*—as well befits a book that is at least in part a guide to living a life. Early in it Smith emphasizes just how much fear of death shapes our lives. Only four pages in we're told "it is miserable, we think, to be deprived of the light of the sun; to be shut out from life and conversation; to be laid in the cold grave, a prey to corruption and the reptiles of the earth." On the next page we're told that this "dread of death" is the "great poison to the happiness" of mankind and "makes us miserable while we are alive."[3] Smith returns to the same theme later, calling death the "king of terrors," noting that "the man who has conquered the fear of death is not likely to lose his presence of mind at the approach of any other natural evil."[4]

Socrates himself, as Smith well knew, has long served as the quintessential example of how mortal man might transcend the terror of death. In *The Theory of Moral Sentiments* Smith himself repeatedly invokes the famous image of Socrates condemned to death by the Athenian jury and calmly preparing to drink the hemlock. In this vein, at one point he holds up Socrates as a model of "heroic magnanimity," painting for us how "the friends of Socrates all wept when he drank the last potion, while he himself expressed the gayest and most cheerful tranquillity."[5] At another point he calls us to witness Socrates' "dazzling splendour," suggesting Socrates might have never enjoyed his "glory" through the ages had his enemies merely "suffered him to die quietly in his bed."[6] And elsewhere he holds up Socrates as an exemplar of courage, classing him among those rare men capable of having "submitted patiently to that death to which the injustice of their fellow-citizens had condemned them."[7]

In all of these instances Socrates shows himself to be a wise and virtuous man of the sort described by Smith. Like the wise and virtuous man, Socrates is capable of exercising the awful virtue of self-command in order to master that most powerful and ungovernable of all self-regarding feelings, the fear of our own dissolution. Yet what enabled Socrates to muster this degree of self-command? His admirers have long regarded his courage before death as inseparable from his commitment to philosophy; in Montaigne's famous study, to philosophize in Socrates' way is nothing less than to learn how to die. But here Smith parts ways with Socrates' admirers. As admirable as his self-command may be, something about Socrates' approach to philosophy troubles Smith. Put too simply, Socrates' philosophy may have liberated him from a fear of death, but it failed to liberate him from other sorts of self-regarding concerns— including especially the love of attention that has been such a focus of our inquiry to this point. In this vein, Smith goes so far as to lump Socrates in with Alexander the Great and Julius Caesar, invoking all three as cases of "excessive self-admiration." Thus Smith's accusation of Socrates: that "amidst the respectful admiration of his followers and disciples, amidst the universal applause of the public," even the truly "great wisdom" of Socrates simply "was not great enough to hinder him from fancying that he had secret and frequent intimations from some invisible and divine Being."[8]

I have to say that I'm not sure, based on what we know from Plato and other ancient writers, that Smith's accusation of Socrates here is entirely fair. Smith is right to note that Socrates frequently spoke to his *daemon*—sort of a pagan version of what is today sometimes called a guardian angel—as Plato makes clear.[9] But the Socrates that Plato depicts is hardly a sycophant whose sense of self-worth depends on having legions of followers, nor is he a deluded enthusiast. So we may do better to look to sources other than Smith if we want the full truth about Socrates. That said, Smith's critique of Socrates casts important light on the problem that lies at the heart of the project of living a life.

Smith here makes a very specific accusation of Socrates. In terms of the categories we've been using, it's that Socrates crossed the line separating those human beings who are "godlike" and human beings who believe themselves to be in touch with the gods. On some level, the suggestion is that Socrates' wisdom, the product of his philosophy, put him on the level of the gods and above other people. This of course runs wholly counter to what Smith thinks the wise and virtuous should never forget: that they are just one of the multitude, no better than any other in it. But it also runs counter to how a wise and virtuous person must live and act, according to Smith. To be wise and virtuous, as we've seen, is to live in such a way that our wisdom informs our virtue, rather than separating us from or absolving us of virtue. Socrates himself was clearly capable of "the most sublime speculation." But Smith believes as much as he believes anything that "nature has not prescribed to us this sublime contemplation as the great business and occupation of our lives."[10] On the contrary (and as we know from chapter 3) he thinks nature has made us for action. And thus however wise they may be, philosophers can't be considered both wise and virtuous if their sublime speculations draw them away from those "active duties" with which nature has charged us.

XXVII

———— ★ ————

"We are led to the belief of a future state, not only by the weaknesses, by the hopes and fears of human nature, but by the noblest and best principles which belong to it, by the love of virtue, and by the abhorrence of vice and injustice."

Or: the love of virtue leads us to, not away from, religious belief.

The wise and virtuous man, as we've seen, is in many ways similar to Socrates. But he's not entirely similar to Socrates. For while the wise and virtuous man shares Socrates' self-command, his commitment to virtue precludes him from pursuing a philosophical life devoted to speculation. But what about that other exemplary life of Ben Franklin's, the life of Jesus?

Unlike Socrates, who appears more than once in *The Theory of Moral Sentiments*, Jesus isn't mentioned once in the text. That said, the religion founded in Jesus' name is, by my count, mentioned three times in *The Theory of Moral Sentiments*.[1] Interestingly, at each of the three times Smith mentions Christianity, he focuses on its idea of love. And this fact, coupled with Smith's own interest in love—an interest we've seen him profess at a number of places—may lead those of us interested in the question of the best life to wonder what place, if any, religion has in this life.

Smith's answer to this question may surprise some people. Smith was of course a leading thinker of the Enlightenment. And the Enlightenment has long been seen as hostile to religion. But that old view of Enlightenment has been much rethought in recent years, thanks to a great deal of recent scholarship illuminating the connections of religion and Enlightenment—connections that debunk an antiquated view of religious orthodoxy and Enlightenment philosophy as mutual enemies in irreconcilable camps.[2] I mention this here because scholars are also now rethinking Smith's understanding of religion. For many years, it was assumed that on matters of religion Smith followed the lead of his friend David Hume, a philosopher famous in his day and ours for heterodoxy. Hume notoriously argued that religious belief could be traced to the most craven and self-interested parts of human nature, and specifically our hopes and fears.[3] But the quotation for this chapter suggests that Smith had a very different view of religion. Indeed this quotation is nothing less than a repudiation of Hume's views on religion. For where Hume traces belief to what is worst in us, Smith, in striking contrast, says that we are led to religious belief by "the noblest and best principles" of human nature—indeed by "the love of virtue" itself.

This is a big claim. In fact, there are several big claims here, and it's probably worth spending a few moments trying to unpack them. First, Smith is making a point here about religion and human nature. Put most simply, Smith's claim is that religion is natural to us—that it is not a foreign construct, imposed on us from on high, but a form of belief that both comes from and fits with the way that we've been made. At the end of the chapter in which we find the quotation for this chapter, Smith refers to what he calls "the natural principles of religion."[4] This locution has long fascinated me. Here though I want to note only that Smith thinks there are religious principles that are natural to us, and foremost among these is "the humble hope and expectation of a life to come"—"a hope and expectation deeply rooted in human nature," and which "can alone support its lofty ideas of its own dignity."[5]

Second, Smith here says that the part of our nature that gives rise to these natural religious principles is "the noblest and best" part. From Hume's day to our own, religion's critics have often argued that believers come to believe out of cowardice, or out of fear, or because they are anxious and worried. But Smith thinks that many people take a different path to religion. They believe not because they want something that will relieve them of their fear or anxiety. They believe because they feel, as he says, "sorrow and compassion for the sufferings of the innocent." They believe, that is—and put in terms of our inquiry—not out of self-interest, but out of concern for others. Specifically, this concern for others, and especially innocent others who suffer at the hands of the wicked and unjust, makes us "naturally appeal to heaven" in the hope that God will ensure justice will be done at last.[6]

This leads to a third key point about Smith's views on religion. I've been using the language of "religion" and "religious belief" throughout this chapter, but we need to be as precise as possible here. Smith, after all, isn't really talking about all the phenomena that properly come under the heading of religion; there's very little theology proper in Smith, and even less discussion of, say, religious ritual and practice. So too when it comes to the range of religious beliefs that he describes. For Smith, the one belief that really matters is that which concerns an omnipotent God who will punish the unjust in an afterlife. That of course is only one among many things that people of faith might have in mind when they profess their faith. But for Smith, this is the belief that most matters, and maybe even the only belief that matters—a position that attests to the degree to which he tended to see religion exclusively through the lens of morality.

In any case, Smith's insistence that we are led to this belief by the love of virtue suggests that he thinks that there is a place for religion in the life of virtue. This places him outside of a way of thinking that emphasizes a tension between these. In my field, political philosophy, this tension is sometimes described as one between "Athens" and "Jerusalem." Athens and Jerusalem are taken to represent two contrasting visions of the good and how it comes to be known: one by reason and philosophy, the other by revelation and faith.[7] I'm not concerned to contest this debate here. But I think it's useful to have on the table, if only to help us appreciate the degree to which Smith conceived his wise and virtuous person as an alternative.

XXVIII

———— ✳ ————

"Upon the whole, I have always considered him, both in his lifetime and since his death, as approaching as nearly to the idea of a perfectly wise and virtuous man, as perhaps the nature of human frailty will permit."

Or: we may be flawed and frail but we can aim high, and Hume's example shows us how.

The wise and virtuous person, as we've seen, aims at perfection. And perfection, we've also seen, is necessarily an abstraction for Smith, since real human beings are too flawed to attain it. But this doesn't mean that we can't come close. Indeed, Smith thinks some real human beings have in fact "nearly approached" it. And foremost among them is none other than his friend David Hume.

Hume died in August 1776, just a few months after the *Wealth of Nations* had been published and a few weeks after the Declaration of Independence had been signed. On the occasion of his death—itself a public event, as many were eager to know how the ostensible atheist would face his demise, absent a belief in the afterlife—Smith took it upon himself to write and publish a celebration of his friend. It appeared in the form of a letter to William Strahan, Hume and Smith's mutual friend and publisher, in which Smith recounted Hume's state of mind in his final days. The quote for this chapter is the final line of this letter.

Smith's letter ultimately brought him a fair amount of grief. To defend one widely reputed as an infidel was to open oneself to the wrath of certain defenders of the faith, and Smith certainly felt this wrath; in a famous line, Smith later remarked about his letter that "a single, and as, I thought a very harmless sheet of paper, which I happened to write concerning the death of our late friend Mr Hume, brought upon me ten times more abuse than the very violent attack I had made upon the whole commercial system of Great Britain."[1] But Smith was the furthest thing from naïve when it came to matters of public opinion on religious matters. One suspects he knew full well what he was getting into when he wrote his letter. So why did he do it? One answer may be that he wanted to teach us something about wisdom and virtue. And indeed there are a number of lessons here about wisdom and virtue, lessons that are both obvious and less obvious.

First and foremost, as readers from Smith's day to ours have long appreciated (and indeed never fail to mention when talking about the letter), the line of the letter that is our focus in this chapter was itself consciously intended to echo the last line of Plato's *Phaedo*, which recounts Socrates' last days.[2] We've already seen (chapter 26) that Smith would have had reason to be interested in the *Phaedo* and its themes in light of his evident interest in Socrates' attitude toward death. In applying Plato's praises of Socrates and his attitude toward death to Hume and his attitude to death, Smith obviously meant to cast his friend as a modern Socrates.

But Smith also sought to do something more. Hume isn't just a Socratic philosopher for Smith. As the closing line says, Hume was more than a philosopher: he was a "wise and virtuous man." And here's where the significance for our study lies.

In substituting Hume for Socrates, Smith means to substitute the excellence of the wise and virtuous man for the excellence of the philosopher. The wise and virtuous man, that is, goes beyond the sort of excellence of the philosopher by at once embodying his excellence and adding to it a new sort of excellence that is distinctive to the wise and virtuous man himself. And in the body of his letter, Smith makes clear just how Hume did this.

In the letter, Smith shows that Hume's claim to being a wise and virtuous man rests on his bringing together of the awful virtues and the amiable virtues. His portrait of Hume particularly emphasizes his friend's awful virtues. Calling attention to Hume's submission to death "with the utmost cheerfulness, and the most perfect complacency and resignation," Smith suggests this resignation was made possible by Hume's "magnanimity and firmness," even as Hume "never affected to make any parade of his magnanimity."[3] In continuing, he further emphasizes the utility of this magnanimous self-command by quoting the words of Hume's doctor Joseph Black, who described his patient in his final days as "'quite free from anxiety'" and dying "'in such a happy composure of mind, that nothing could exceed it.'"[4] And for his part, Smith especially emphasizes Hume's "cheerfulness"—a word he uses no fewer than seven times to describe his friend in this short letter.

In these lines Smith brings together several of the key themes of our study to this point, including the nobility of self-command, the relationship of tranquility to happiness, and the superiority of praiseworthiness to praise. But for all this, Hume's real greatness—and indeed his claim to wisdom and virtue—lies elsewhere. What makes Hume especially admirable in Smith's eyes is that he manages to combine with these awful virtues certain amiable virtues. In this vein, Smith notably says of Hume that "even in the lowest state of his fortune, his great and necessary frugality never hindered him from exercising, upon proper occasions, acts both of charity and generosity." At the same time, Smith notes, "the extreme gentleness of his nature never weakened either the firmness of his mind, or the steadiness of his resolutions." The key point here is that Hume brought together "great and amiable qualities" in a way that led his temper to be "happily balanced."[5]

With this in place, we can see why Smith might have been willing to run the risks of publicly celebrating Hume in spite of his reputation in matters of religion. In Smith's hands, Hume stands as a model not just of philosophical excellence but of the excellence of a wise and virtuous person, the person whose single character combines the awful virtues of self-command and magnanimity with the amiable virtues of charity and generosity—the person whose way of living is at once good for himself and good for others. But even so, there's an issue still unresolved. Smith, after all, took it upon himself to defend one who was reputed, at least by some, to be an atheist. Just what might this suggest about Smith's own beliefs?

Many have taken Smith's letter as an endorsement of Hume and his beliefs, and his religious infidelity in particular. The most complete study of their friendship indeed sees Smith's praise of Hume as "difficult to read as anything other than a deliberate challenge to the devout."[6] But there may be another way to read this. Smith clearly admired Hume for his character. Yet admiring someone for his character isn't quite the same as endorsing his ideas. Today we often find it hard to distinguish these. In our age, opinions are often taken as proxy for values, and holding differing opinions (especially political opinions) is often taken as evidence of suspect values. We shun people who don't share our opinions on matters we think crucial, blocking and unfriending them on social media and avoiding them in real life. But Smith, living in an age of enlightenment and personally committed to ideals of respect and toleration, took a different and more generous perspective. For in the end, Smith and Hume, I think, had different ideas about religion.[7] But for all that, Smith was able to disaggregate his friend's ideas on religion from the virtues of his character, and this was what enabled him to admire and celebrate his friend's character even though some of his friend's opinions made him pause. Smith, that is, was able to do something that many of us find it difficult to do today: namely to celebrate all that he and his friend shared in common even in the face of real disagreements that might lead lesser people to break all ties to each other. Smith's letter thus offers us a glimpse in action of a sort of admiration and respect that is increasingly uncommon today—and indeed one that suggests we may have as much to learn about wisdom and virtue from the example of the author of the letter as from the example of its subject.

XXIX

✴

"Every part of nature, when attentively surveyed, equally
demonstrates the providential care of its Author, and
we may admire the wisdom and goodness of God
even in the weakness and folly of man."

*Or: beyond the wisdom and virtue of man lies the wisdom
and goodness of God.*

Our inquiry into the challenges of living a life has led us to the
life of the wise and virtuous man. But beyond the wisdom and
virtue of man lies what Smith here calls "the wisdom and
goodness of God." And next to the wisdom and goodness of
God, the wisdom and virtue of man seem less apparent than
"the weakness and folly of man."[1] Setting man next to God, as
Smith does here, reminds us just how far removed even the
best of men are from absolute perfection.

But putting it this way also prompts a question. Namely:
what sort of relationship is fitting between a wise and virtuous
person and a wise and good God? Here and elsewhere Smith
suggests that part of a human being's task is to develop a proper
conception of this relationship. This may be one of the most
difficult tasks for a wise and virtuous person to accomplish,
and so we can't close this inquiry into Smith's philosophy of
living without at least a brief consideration of it.

Who then is God, and what role does he have in our lives? It would of course take a theologian to do justice to this question, and Smith is not a theologian. Even to do justice to the human idea of God, aside from any consideration of God's existence or being, we'd need an epistemologist, and Smith is not an epistemologist. But Smith is a careful student of what is sometimes called moral psychology—that is, the field of interaction between our ideas and cognitions and our moral sentiments and behaviors—and it is from this point of view that he takes up the question of the idea of God. In this vein, he tells us that "the idea of that divine Being, whose benevolence and wisdom have, from all eternity, contrived and conducted the immense machine of the universe, so as at all times to produce the greatest possible quantity of happiness, is certainly of all the objects of human contemplation by far the most sublime."[2] Now, as we've already noted at several different points, Smith doesn't think that contemplation, however sublime, can be the sole end of human activity; we were made for action, as we know. But in making this claim about the idea of God, Smith suggests that a certain kind of idea of God can in fact promote our moral action.

This is so for at least two reasons. First, Smith thinks a certain idea of God can help its possessor to act out of a regard for praiseworthiness and blameworthiness rather than out of the more common human regard for praise and blame. We remember from earlier that Smith thinks the essential figure in this process is the impartial spectator; a wise and virtuous person cares more for the judgments of this impartial spectator than for the praise and blame of actual spectators. Actual spectators are often imperfect, as we know, and the impartial spectator is an improvement on these. But the impartial spectator is itself merely an imperfect representative of the genuinely perfect judgment that Smith thinks God alone possesses. This in part explains why those misunderstood by the world are often religious, as religion "alone can tell them, that it is of little importance what man may think of their conduct, while the all-seeing Judge of the world approves of it."[3]

The idea of God as the "all-seeing Judge of the world" can thus help to bolster our fortitude and resolve to act morally in those instances where we face the disapprobation of the world. But for Smith, God is the creator and governor of the world as well as the judge of the world—the one who "from all eternity" has "contrived and conducted the immense machine of the universe." Now, in making this claim, Smith follows the lead of the ancient Stoics, who, as he notes, regarded the world as "governed by the all-ruling providence of a wise, powerful, and good God," one in which "the vices and follies of mankind" played "as necessary" a role as "their wisdom or their virtue."[4]

Awed by the immensity and complexity of this machine, the wise man, the Stoics taught, was expected to display "a reverential submission" to "that benevolent wisdom which directs all the events of human life."[5] Is this Smith's view too? Lots of ink has been spilled on the question of Smith's Stoicism, but I can't adjudicate the whole of that dispute here.[6] Instead, I'll end this inquiry into Smith's philosophy of living by noting just one point of agreement with the Stoics. The Stoics, Smith says, taught that wisdom leads to an appreciation of one's place in our good and providentially ordered world. It also leads us to want to contribute to the order and goodness of world through our own actions. But this is Smith's point as well. "By acting according to the dictates of our moral faculties, we necessarily pursue the most effectual means for promoting the happiness of mankind, and may therefore be said, in some sense, to co-operate with the Deity, and to advance as far as in our power the plan of Providence."[7] The end of our goodness thus isn't simply our own happiness but the promotion of the happiness of all, and thereby God's will, here on earth.

EPILOGUE

✳

Why Smith Now?

Adam Smith, I've sought to show, has a philosophy of living that deserves the attention of those concerned to live as well as possible. Yet even if we're persuaded that Smith has something to offer on this front, he's of course far from the only thinker in our tradition who has something to say about such matters. So what makes his philosophy of living any more worth our attention than many others that we've inherited? I think three answers can be given to this question, and I'll end this book by laying them out.

Traditionally there have been two sources of guidance to which those interested in the question of the good life have turned: religion and philosophy. On the former front, the world's great spiritual and faith traditions all offer counsel on wise living from which many have drawn meaning. On the latter, the philosophers of ancient Greece and ancient Rome in particular have long served as sources of insight into what makes a life worth living, and by what standards we might judge a way of living to be good or bad.

Yet these traditional sources of wisdom seem unavailable to many among us today, or at least they are unavailable in the same sense in which they were available to previous generations for whom they had been indispensable anchors. As has been noted, we today live in a secular age.[1] Even as many of us today live lives of faith, it is yet the case the organizing categories of our modern world are no longer those of the religious worldview. So too, Plato and Aristotle and the Stoics are still read by many today. Yet modern science has rendered implausible to most the metaphysical grounds on which their judgments of better and worse lives were grounded. So not everyone today has access to the wisdom available in these traditions and these texts—a point I appreciate, even as a person of faith who makes a living teaching and writing about these and related thinkers and traditions.

All of this leads me to think that we would do well to broaden our search for wise guides to living beyond these traditions and texts. What we need are guides who "speak our language"—that is, guides who not only provide us with insight and counsel, but can do so within the framework of the beliefs and categories that shape our world. This is one reason why Smith is a useful guide for us today. Smith drew deeply from the wells of antiquity and Christianity, as I hope will be evident from my account of his thought above. But even in embracing many ancient and Christian teachings, he recognized that they need to be developed if they are to remain alive for our modern world. Much of his genius as a moral philosopher lies in his abilities on this front, and much of his value as a guide to our questions lies in this capacity to articulate wisdom in a language we today can understand.

There is also a second reason why Smith is a useful guide for us today. Our world is simply not the world of medieval Christian Europe or ancient pagan Greece. That is surely obvious enough. But this fact is of crucial importance for the particular problem of living life well in our world. For our world not only lacks access to certain ideas and beliefs that were foundational to these previous worlds, but also comes with a set of challenges to living a good life that are all its own. As a result, in trying to live our lives today we face challenges very different from those faced by citizens of the ancient Greek *polis*, or citizens of the earthly city of man aware of its distance from the heavenly city of God.

These challenges are many and complex, but it is worth reminding ourselves here of a few of those discussed above. Our world, for example, values the trappings of wealth and fortune, the signs of success in modern markets. Yet while some wealth and fortune seems necessary for happiness, past a certain point more wealth and fortune doesn't lead to more happiness, as we all know (and much social science research confirms).[2] So too, and as we have seen Smith emphasize, our world values signs of esteem and recognition: signs we can now more easily and precisely measure thanks to the metrics of social media. Yet these too seem increasingly unlikely to lead to happiness. And perhaps most interestingly: many in our world claim to value happiness above all else. But at least one effect of the pursuit of happiness is that those in its grip often become remarkably self-centered and less attuned to the happiness and well-being of others.

These features of our world are tied in large part to the emergence of what we today call capitalist society, and Smith himself called "commercial society." Now, the goal of this book of course has not been to defend or decry capitalism. That has been often enough done by others. But as we've seen, Smith himself defended commercial society on the grounds of the significant material benefits it brings to the poorest among us, and on this front history (at least to this point) has vindicated him. The last two hundred years have seen remarkable amelioration of global poverty—indeed to such a degree that in 2016 the United Nations adopted as the first of its seventeen Sustainable Development Goals a total eradication of global extreme poverty by 2030.[3] We cannot but be grateful for the progress that has enabled us to be able even to conceive of this goal. But neither should we allow these welcome gains to blind us to the costs at which they have been bought. And if the gains are material, the costs are often moral, and include, among others, rising senses of selfishness, isolation, and anxiety—phenomena pernicious to social trust and political order, but also to our efforts to live well.

Smith understood as well as any how commercial society generates these benefits and these challenges alike. A philosopher of the Enlightenment, fortunate to have lived before the age of hyperspecialization, he combined the economist's understanding of the mechanisms of market society with the ethicist's appreciation of the challenges of market society. And this remarkable (and remarkably balanced) appreciation of market society's opportunities as well as its challenges shaped his philosophy of living. As a result, he has what an economist would call a "comparative advantage" over other guides to wise living with whom we might be familiar. Thus the second reason why he is so useful to us today. Smith wrote for our world, in two senses. As we saw above, his philosophy is grounded in the language and concepts of our world. But in developing this philosophy, he also sought to respond to the unique challenges that our modern commercial world presents to living life well.

There's also at least one other reason why we do well to turn to Smith for guidance. This concerns the type of philosopher he sought to be. As we saw, Smith made his living as a professor of moral philosophy, serving as a distinguished teacher at his alma mater, the University of Glasgow. But Smith would be a poor fit in most departments of philosophy today. Today's professional philosophy is a specialized and technical field. To outsiders its questions are no more recognizable than questions in advanced mathematics or physics. In part, Smith would have welcomed this: a champion of the way in which divided and specialized labor increases productivity, he himself noted the payoffs of specialization for philosophy.[4] But he also knew that what has been lost amidst this specialization, as several other prominent philosophers have more recently emphasized, are the ancient questions about the nature of the good life and how to live it.[5] Yet it is these that Smith himself thinks are the heart of philosophy itself.

Moral philosophy, he thus explains, has two tasks. One is to identify the "power or faculty of the mind" that enables us to make judgments. Now, if that sounds like a merely academic or technical question to you, you'll be happy to know that Smith thought so too. He himself calls it "a mere matter of philosophical curiosity," which, while "of the greatest importance in speculation, is of none in practice."[6] This is not to say he thought it wholly unimportant; much of his own book on moral philosophy (and most of the books that have been written about his moral philosophy) is dedicated to it. But for all that, he insists that the first task of moral philosophy is to answer a different question. That question, as he has it, is: "wherein does virtue consist? Or what is the tone of temper, and tenour of conduct, which constitutes the excellent and praise-worthy character?"[7]

Smith's philosophy of living is shaped by his interest in this ancient question of what it means to have an "excellent and praise-worthy character." Yet his way of answering this ancient question is very modern. A member in good standing of the Enlightenment, Smith is committed to empirical methods: observation and study of real data. His vision, and indeed the vision of the wise and virtuous man, of the perfect and the praiseworthy and the noble and the honorable is grounded in his study of real people in the real world, as we've seen. Both Smith and his wise and virtuous man are always observers— "spectators"—describing details of what they've seen in different men and moments. This approach is part of what makes

Smith's book so readable, even today. And what is perhaps especially remarkable about Smith's book is the way in which he holds up these insights for us, his readers, to see. In so doing he trains us to become good spectators in our own right, better able to see and recognize good acts, good characters, and good lives when we come across them—in Smith's words, he aims "to make us know the original when we meet with it."[8]

But there's also another part to Smith's method. Smith not only sees: he also reflects on what he sees. In particular, he reflects on how all the different little things that he's seen can be seen as going together. This is especially evident in his economics. Smith of course is famous today for his invisible hand. But the invisible hand is a metaphor, and specifically a metaphor for what Smith himself calls the "system of natural liberty."[9] This system, like many other systems that Smith describes in his writings, is an extremely complex machine that coordinates the discrete activities of untold parts. Smith's genius as an economist lay in his capacity to describe how all of these discrete parts hang together—to make visible the many resemblances between them that are "invisible" at first glance.

Reflection of this sort uncovers connections. And this same method is at work in Smith's moral philosophy. Just as Smith's economics shows how the discrete phenomena that we see before us can be understood as connected in a single, integrated whole, Smith's philosophy of living shows us how the different parts of a life can be seen as hanging together. This is partly why his ethics focuses on helping us to recognize "the excellent and praise-worthy character" and not simply on classifying discrete actions as right or wrong. For this excellent and praise-worthy character, like the life it determines, is a unity, the sum of a staggering multitude of experiences and emotions. As such, it takes a trained eye to see it, to appreciate it, and to live it, this life of action and reflection, wisdom and virtue.

Table of Quotations

———— ★ ————

Texts and Further Reading

——— ✶ ———

References to Smith's published books are to the Penguin Classics editions: *The Theory of Moral Sentiments*, ed. Ryan Patrick Hanley (Penguin, 2009), and the *Wealth of Nations*, ed. Andrew S. Skinner, 2 vols. (Penguin, 1999).

The standard scholarly edition of Smith's works is published in hardcover by Oxford University Press and paperback by the Liberty Fund. Known as the Glasgow Edition, this version includes Smith's correspondence and student notes of his courses on rhetoric and jurisprudence as well as critical editions of his published texts. I have cited this edition in referencing Smith's *Lectures on Jurisprudence*, ed. R. L. Meek, D. D. Raphael, and P. G. Stein (Liberty Fund, 1982) and the *Correspondence of Adam Smith*, ed. E. C. Mossner and I. S. Ross (Liberty Fund, 1987).

We are fortunate to have several excellent biographies of Smith. Among the best and most accessible of these are Nicholas Phillipson, *Adam Smith: An Enlightened Life* (Yale, 2010), and James Buchan, *The Authentic Adam Smith* (Norton, 2006). The authoritative and by far the most comprehensive biography is I. S. Ross, *The Life of Adam Smith*, 2nd ed. (Oxford, 2010).

Several volumes of essays provide helpful introductions to Smith's thought. I was fortunate to be able to gather an outstanding set of contributors who provide brief and helpful guides to Smith's ideas in *Adam Smith: His Life, Thought, and Legacy*, ed. Ryan Patrick Hanley (Princeton, 2016). Several other collections of essays also deserve recommendation, including especially *The Cambridge Companion to Adam Smith*, ed. Knud Haakonssen (Cambridge, 2006), and *The Oxford Handbook of Adam Smith*, ed. Christopher J. Berry, Maria Pia Paganelli, and Craig Smith (Oxford, 2013).

For overviews of Smith's thought as a whole, readers would do well to begin with Jerry Z. Muller, *Adam Smith in His Time and Ours* (Princeton, 1995), and Christopher J. Berry, *Adam Smith: A Very Short Introduction* (Oxford, 2019). And Jesse Norman's recent book *Adam Smith: Father of Economics* (Basic Books, 2018) provides an accurate, attractive, and accessible overview of Smith's ideas on ethics and economics and why they matter today.

Those seeking an introduction to Smith's economics as presented in the *Wealth of Nations* will benefit from Jerry Evensky, *Adam Smith's* Wealth of Nations*: A Reader's Guide* (Cambridge, 2015), as well as Samuel Fleischacker, *On Adam Smith's* Wealth of Nations*: A Philosophical Companion* (Princeton, 2004).

A short and older but still valuable introduction to *The Theory of Moral Sentiments* can be found in Joseph Cropsey, *Polity and Economy* (Martinus Nijhoff, 1957). Other classic studies of Smith's moral and political thought include A. L. Macfie, *The Individual in Society* (Allen and Unwin, 1967), T. D. Campbell, *Adam Smith's Science of Morals* (Allen and Unwin, 1971), J. R. Lindgren, *The Social Philosophy of Adam Smith* (Martinus Nijhoff, 1973), and Donald Winch, *Adam Smith's Politics* (Cambridge, 1978). More recently, see D. D. Raphael, *The Impartial Spectator: Adam Smith's Moral Philosophy* (Oxford, 2007), which provides a (sometimes polemical) overview of several of Smith's key ideas. Russ Roberts provides a popularization of some of Smith's ideas about ethics in *How Adam Smith Can Change Your Life* (Penguin, 2014).

My own thinking on a number of themes in Smith's philosophy has been shaped by my sustained engagement with the extensive specialized scholarship. Several of these works deserve particular recommendation here, as both specialized and less specialized readers of *The Theory of Moral Sentiments* can benefit from them.

Smith's views on self-interest (the subject of chapter 1 in this volume) are nicely surveyed in Eugene Heath's essay "Adam Smith and Self-Interest" in the *Oxford Handbook of Adam Smith*. Useful overviews of the prehistory of self-interest can be found in Milton L. Myers, *The Soul of Modern Economic Man: Ideas of Self-Interest, Thomas Hobbes to Adam Smith* (Chicago, 1983), and Pierre Force, *Self-Interest Before Adam Smith* (Cambridge, 2003).

Smith's approach to egoism and altruism (a topic discussed in chapter 2) is nicely illuminated by Vernon L. Smith and Bart J. Wilson in *Humanomics: Moral Sentiments and the Wealth of Nations for the Twenty-First Century* (Cambridge, 2019). Another must-read is Vernon Smith's classic essay "The Two Faces of Adam Smith," *Southern Economic Journal* 65 (1998).

Smith's concept of sympathy (chapter four) has been examined by many scholars; among the best studies is Fonna Forman-Barzilai, *Adam Smith and the Circles of Sympathy* (Cambridge, 2010). The history of the concept of sympathy both before and after Smith is surveyed in *Sympathy: A History*, ed. Eric Schliesser (Oxford, 2015); see also Michael Frazer, *The Enlightenment of Sympathy* (Oxford, 2010). On the ways in which Smith's models of sympathy exchange shape his ideas of economic exchange, see especially James Otteson, *Adam Smith's Marketplace of Life* (Cambridge, 2002).

Many scholars have appreciated the role that imagination (chapters 4 and 5) plays in Smith's system; I have learned the most on this front from the masterful treatment in Charles L. Griswold, Jr., *Adam Smith and the Virtues of Enlightenment* (Cambridge, 1999).

Among the first studies to call attention to Smith's concern for the poor (chapter 5) was Istvan Hont and Michael Ignatieff's "Needs and Justice in the *Wealth of Nations*: An Introductory Essay" in their important volume *Wealth and Virtue* (Cambridge, 1983). Since that essay, the books by Muller and Evensky and Fleischacker cited above have all done much to deepen our appreciation of this side of Smith's concerns.

Smith's interests in happiness and bettering our condition (chapters 5, 6, and 8) have received a great deal of recent attention. Among the best recent studies is the article by Dennis Rasmussen, "Does 'Bettering Our Condition' Really Make Us Better Off?," *American Political Science Review* 100 (2006).

On *Das Adam Smith Problem* (chapter 7), see above all Leonidas Montes, "*Das Adam Smith Problem*: Its Origins, the Stages of the Current Debate, and One Implication for Our Understanding of Sympathy," *Journal of the History of Economic Thought* 25 (2003).

A helpful guide to Smith's views on corruption (chapters 7 and 9) can be found in Lisa Hill's article, "Adam Smith and the Theme of Corruption," *Review of Politics* 68 (2006). Relatedly, comparisons of Smith to Rousseau and Marx (both also mentioned in chapter 9) abound. On Marx and Smith, see especially R. L. Meek, *Smith, Marx, and After* (Chapman and Hall, 1977), and Spencer Pack, *Capitalism as a Moral System* (Edward Elgar, 1991). On Rousseau and Smith, see especially Rasmussen, *The Problems and Promise of Commercial Society: Adam Smith's Response to Rousseau* (Penn State, 2008), and Griswold, *Jean-Jacques Rousseau and Adam Smith: A Philosophical Encounter* (Routledge, 2018).

Smith's ideas on friendship (chapter 10) are helpfully explored in several excellent articles, including Douglas J. Den Uyl and Griswold, "Adam Smith on Friendship and Love," *Review of Metaphysics* 49 (1996), and Hill and Peter McCarthy, "On Friendship and *Necessitudo* in Adam Smith," *History of the Human Sciences* 17 (2004).

I have long been fascinated by Smith's treatment of anxiety (chapters 10 and 11). The only study devoted to it that I know of is R. F. Brissenden, "Authority, Guilt, and Anxiety in *The Theory of Moral Sentiments*," *Texas Studies in Literature and Language* 11 (1969).

The central themes of Smith's jurisprudence lectures (chapter 11) are helpfully surveyed by Knud Haakonssen in "The Lectures on Jurisprudence," in *Adam Smith: His Life, Thought, and Legacy*. Several studies have compared Smith to Aristotle; I have learned a great deal especially from Martin Calkins and Patricia Werhane, "Adam Smith, Aristotle, and the Virtues of Commerce," *Journal of Value Inquiry* 32 (1998), and Laurence Berns, "Aristotle and Adam Smith on Justice: Cooperation between Ancients and Moderns?," *Review of Metaphysics* 48 (1994).

Smith's treatment of justice (chapter 12) has been examined by many scholars, including several already recommended in this bibliography. The larger significance of his concept of justice is well developed in Haakonssen, *The Science of a Legislator* (Cambridge, 1981). I have learned much about Smith's understanding of the relationship of justice to resentment from Pack and Schliesser, "Smith's Humean Criticism of Hume's Account of the Origin of Justice," *Journal of the History of Philosophy* 44 (2006).

Love (chapter 13) has not tended to be a focal point of Smith scholarship. But in addition to the helpful article by

Den Uyl and Griswold mentioned above, see also Martha Nussbaum, *Upheavals of Thought* (Cambridge, 2001), and Lauren Brubaker, "'A Particular Turn or Habit of the Imagination': Adam Smith on Love, Friendship, and Philosophy," in *Love and Friendship*, ed. Eduardo Velásquez (Lexington, 2003).

Smith's commitment to pluralism (chapter 14) has received increased attention in recent years. In this vein, see especially Jack Russell Weinstein, *Adam Smith's Pluralism: Rationality, Education, and the Moral Sentiments* (Yale, 2013), and Michael B. Gill, "Moral Pluralism in Smith and His Contemporaries," *Revue internationale de philosophie* 68 (2014).

Chapter 15 mentions Smith's notorious man of system. Many commentators have appreciated the significance of this concept for Smith's political thought; an especially lively account is given in F. A. Hayek, "Adam Smith's Message in Today's Language," *Daily Telegraph*, 9 March 1976; also helpful is Craig Smith, *Adam Smith's Political Philosophy* (Routledge, 2006).

Many commentators have noted Smith's distinction between the love of praise and the love of praiseworthiness (chapters 16 and 25). In addition to the treatment to be found in the book of Vernon Smith and Bart Wilson cited above, see now Sveinung Sivertsen, "Love Redirected: On Adam Smith's Love of Praiseworthiness," *Journal of Scottish Philosophy* 15 (2017).

In addition to Raphael's book, cited above, Smith's theory of the impartial spectator (chapter 17) is insightfully examined in several studies of Smith's idea of judgment, including especially Fleischacker, *A Third Concept of Liberty: Judgment and Freedom in Kant and Adam Smith* (Princeton, 1999). Also valuable are Karen Valihora's article, "Judgement of Judgement: Adam Smith's *Theory of Moral Sentiments*," *British Journal of Aesthetics* 41 (2001), and Vivienne Brown's chapter

"Intersubjectivity and Moral Judgment in Adam Smith's *Theory of Moral Sentiments*," in *Intersubjectivity and Objectivity in Adam Smith and Edmund Husserl,* ed. Christel Fricke and Dagfinn Føllesdal (Ontos, 2012).

Smith's commitment to principles of equality and dignity (chapters 18 and 19) is now better appreciated than ever thanks to several studies, including Iain McLean, *Adam Smith, Radical and Egalitarian* (Palgrave Macmillan, 2006), Remy Debes, "Adam Smith on Dignity and Equality," *British Journal for the History of Philosophy* 20 (2012), Lisa Herzog, *Inventing the Market: Smith, Hegel, and Political Theory* (Oxford, 2013), and Elizabeth Anderson, "Adam Smith and Equality," in *Adam Smith: His Life, Thought, and Legacy.* David Levy and Sandra Peart have written illuminatingly about the significance of the porter and philosopher; see their introductory essay in their volume *The Street Porter and the Philosopher: Conversations on Analytical Egalitarianism* (Michigan, 2008).

Smith's theory of virtue (chapter 21) has been helpfully illuminated in several works, including esp. Montes, *Adam Smith in Context* (Palgrave Macmillan, 2004). Smith's ideas on the virtues also play a prominent role in Deirdre McCloskey, *The Bourgeois Virtues: Ethics for an Age of Commerce* (Chicago, 2006).

Those interested in how the life of philosophy comports with a life of active virtue (chapters 23 and 26) will find a great deal of food for thought in Eric Schliesser's recent book *Adam Smith: Systematic Philosopher and Public Thinker* (Oxford, 2017).

Smith's relationship to ancient thinkers such as Socrates and Plato and the Stoics (chapters 26 and 29) has been examined by a number of scholars, but most comprehensively by Gloria Vivenza, *Adam Smith and the Classics* (Oxford, 2001). Andrew J. Corsa's article "Modern Greatness of Soul in Hume and Smith," *Ergo* 2 (2015) insightfully examines Hume's and Smith's reinterpretations of "Socratic magnanimity."

Smith's friendship with Hume and his engagement with Hume's ideas (chapter 28) has long been of interest to scholars. The most recent and comprehensive treatment is Rasmussen, *The Infidel and the Professor: David Hume, Adam Smith, and the Friendship That Shaped Modern Thought* (Princeton, 2017). Serious readers will also want to consult Rasmussen's new edition of relevant texts: *Adam Smith and the Death of David Hume: The Letter to Strahan and Related Texts* (Lexington, 2018). Eric Schliesser also provides an insightful treatment of Smith's letter in "The Obituary of a Vain Philosopher: Adam Smith's Reflections on Hume's Life," *Hume Studies* 29 (2003).

Smith's religious and theological commitments (chapters 27 to 29) have recently emerged as points for debate among specialist scholars; compare, for example, Gavin Kennedy, *An Authentic Account of Adam Smith* (Palgrave Macmillan, 2017), with the volume *Adam Smith as Theologian*, ed. Paul Oslington (Routledge, 2011). A helpful point of entry into these debates can be found is Gordon Graham's essay "Adam Smith and Religion," in *Adam Smith: His Life, Thought, and Legacy*.

Finally, I've written at much greater length elsewhere about most of the themes addressed in this book. Many of these treatments come in various essays and articles, but those interested in my fuller arguments, as well as how I situate them within the extensive secondary literature debates, can find many of them in two of my books: *Adam Smith and the Character of Virtue* (Cambridge, 2009), and *Love's Enlightenment: Rethinking Charity in Modernity* (Cambridge, 2017).

Notes

———— ✳ ————

Introduction

1. My understanding of what it means to have a "philosophy of living" owes much to both Alexander Nehamas, *The Art of Living* (California, 1998), and Pierre Hadot, *Philosophy as a Way of Life* (Blackwell, 1995). My thoughts on the good life are also deeply indebted to the teaching and writing of Leon Kass; see esp. his *Leading a Worthy Life: Finding Meaning in Modern Times* (Encounter, 2017).

2. Jordan Peterson, *12 Rules for Life: An Antidote to Chaos* (Penguin Random House, 2018).

3. Dugald Stewart, "Account of the Life and Writings of Adam Smith, LL.D.," in *Essays on Philosophical Subjects*, ed. W.P.D. Wightman and J. C. Bryce (Liberty Fund, 1982), 291.

4. Woodrow Wilson, *An Old Master, and Other Political Essays* (C. Scribner's Sons, 1893), 17–18.

5. Readers interested in this side of Smith will do especially well to consult Russ Roberts, *How Adam Smith Can Change Your Life* (Penguin, 2014), which aims to present Smith's advice on "what the good life is and how to achieve it" (2) by recasting *The Theory of Moral Sentiments* into a "digestible form" for readers unlikely to "get around to reading all of the original" (10).

6. Knud Haakonssen and Donald Winch, "The Legacy of Adam Smith," in *The Cambridge Companion to Adam Smith*, ed. Haakonssen (Cambridge, 2006), 385.

7. Even though the way I present Smith's ideas here is unique, most of my discrete claims are generally accepted among scholars. When I do make claims outside the mainstream or on points where there is significant debate, I indicate these in notes.

8. Readers seeking more comprehensive introductions to Smith's life and thought will do well to consult the books by Phillipson and Buchan and Norman listed in the suggestions for further reading.

I. On Self-Interest

1. George Stigler, "Smith's Travels on the Ship of State," in *Essays on Adam Smith*, ed. Andrew S. Skinner and Thomas Wilson (Oxford, 1975), 237.
2. *Theory of Moral Sentiments*, 250.
3. *Theory of Moral Sentiments*, 214–15.
4. *Theory of Moral Sentiments*, 357.
5. *Theory of Moral Sentiments*, 200–201.
6. See also *Theory of Moral Sentiments*, 258.

II. On Caring for Others

1. For an especially stimulating rereading of Smith's views on altruism and egoism from a social scientific perspective, see Vernon L. Smith and Bart J. Wilson, *Humanomics: Moral Sentiments and the Wealth of Nations for the Twenty-First Century* (Cambridge, 2019).
2. Not all philosophers agree that establishing unity in one's life is a desirable goal; for an important counter to the view I'm developing here, see Charles Larmore, "The Idea of a Life Plan," *Social Philosophy and Policy* 16 (1999).
3. *Theory of Moral Sentiments*, 317.

IV. On Imagination

1. *Theory of Moral Sentiments*, 133.
2. On the dynamics of honor cultures, see Tamler Sommers, *Why Honor Matters* (Basic Books, 2018). Smith himself was fascinated by the court of Louis XIV; see, for example, *Theory of Moral Sentiments*, 67–68.

V. On Bettering Our Condition

1. *Wealth of Nations*, 1:441.
2. *Theory of Moral Sentiments*, 63.
3. *Theory of Moral Sentiments*, 62.
4. *Theory of Moral Sentiments*, 212.

VI. On Miseries and Disorders

1. The classic study in psychology is Philip Brickman et al., "Lottery Winners and Accident Victims: Is Happiness Relative?," *Journal of Personality and Social Psychology* 36 (1978); more recently, see Bruno Frey, *Economics of Happiness* (Springer, 2018).
2. *Theory of Moral Sentiments*, 172.
3. *Theory of Moral Sentiments*, 172.

4. *Theory of Moral Sentiments*, 173.
5. *Theory of Moral Sentiments*, 211–13.

VII. On the Healthy Mind

1. *Theory of Moral Sentiments*, 215.
2. *Wealth of Nations*, 1:109–19.
3. *Wealth of Nations*, 2:374.
4. *Wealth of Nations*, 2:374–75.
5. For Smith's views on institutions, see Nathan Rosenberg, "Some Institutional Aspects of the *Wealth of Nations*," *Journal of Political Economy* 68 (1960); and esp. Jerry Muller, *Adam Smith in His Time and Ours* (Princeton, 1995).

VIII. On Tranquility and Pleasure

1. *Theory of Moral Sentiments*, 173.
2. *Theory of Moral Sentiments*, 215.

IX. On Worshipping Wealth

1. For a contemporary defense of the benefits of this approach, see Diana Mutz, *Hearing the Other Side: Deliberative vs. Participatory Democracy* (Cambridge, 2006).
2. See, e.g., Denise Schaeffer, *Rousseau on Education, Freedom and Judgment* (Penn State, 2013); and Laurence Cooper, *Rousseau, Nature, and the Problem of the Good Life* (Penn State, 1999).
3. Jean-Jacques Rousseau, *Emile, or On Education*, trans. Allan Bloom (Basic Books, 1979), 41.

X. On Friendship

1. *Theory of Moral Sentiments*, 59.
2. *Theory of Moral Sentiments*, 30.
3. *Theory of Moral Sentiments*, 265.

XI. On Pleasure

1. *Lectures on Jurisprudence*, 497.
2. Aristotle, *Politics*, 1253a1–19.
3. *Theory of Moral Sentiments*, 36.

XII. On Hatred and Anger

1. *Theory of Moral Sentiments*, 47.
2. *Theory of Moral Sentiments*, 49.
3. See, for example, *Theory of Moral Sentiments*, 39–42.
4. *Theory of Moral Sentiments*, 92 and 94.

XIII. On Being Loved

1. See, e.g., Nancy Folbre, *The Invisible Heart: Economics and Family Values* (New Press, 2001).
2. *Theory of Moral Sentiments*, 49.
3. *Theory of Moral Sentiments*, 52.

XIV. On Loving

1. *Wealth of Nations*, 1:118–19.
2. The debate over whether Smith is better understood as a normative philosopher or as a descriptive social scientist has long been prominent in Smith scholarship. I subscribe to the former position; a classic statement of the latter is T. D. Campbell, *Adam Smith's Science of Morals* (Allen and Unwin, 1971); more recently, see Fonna Forman-Barzilai, *Adam Smith and the Circles of Sympathy* (Cambridge, 2010).
3. I have in mind here especially Isaiah Berlin's famous defense of "value pluralism." For a helpful recent overview, see esp. George Crowder, "Pluralism, Relativism, and Liberalism," in *The Cambridge Companion to Isaiah Berlin*, ed. Steven B. Smith and Joshua L. Cherniss (Cambridge, 2018).
4. *Theory of Moral Sentiments*, 252–54.

XV. On Flourishing

1. *Theory of Moral Sentiments*, 103–4.
2. *Theory of Moral Sentiments*, 275–76.
3. *Theory of Moral Sentiments*, 104.
4. My focus on Smith's comments on love and flourishing here differs from a common reading of these passages that emphasizes Smith's sharp distinction between justice and benevolence. For an early articulation of this position that has received frequent echo, see Joseph Cropsey, *Polity and Economy* (Martinus Nijhoff, 1957), 32–33.
5. *Theory of Moral Sentiments*, 104.

XVI. On Being Lovely

1. *Theory of Moral Sentiments*, 140.
2. *Theory of Moral Sentiments*, 143.
3. *Theory of Moral Sentiments*, 136.

XVII. On Seeing Ourselves

1. *Theory of Moral Sentiments*, 182.
2. *Theory of Moral Sentiments*, 133.
3. *Theory of Moral Sentiments*, 182.
4. *Theory of Moral Sentiments*, 157.

XVIII. On Dignity

1. *Theory of Moral Sentiments*, 161.
2. *Theory of Moral Sentiments*, 159.
3. *Theory of Moral Sentiments*, 101.
4. *Theory of Moral Sentiments*, 166–67.

XIX. On Equality

1. *Wealth of Nations*, 1:120.
2. Max Weber, "Politics as a Vocation," in *From Max Weber: Essays in Sociology*, ed. H. H. Gerth and C. Wright Mills (Routledge, 1991), 116.
3. Plato, *Republic*, 414b–415c.

XX. On Choice

1. *Theory of Moral Sentiments*, 74.
2. *Theory of Moral Sentiments*, 74.
3. *Theory of Moral Sentiments*, 305.
4. *Theory of Moral Sentiments*, 294–95.
5. I am anticipated by Russ Roberts, who likewise speaks of the "less traveled" road in this context; see *How Adam Smith Can Change Your Life*, 112–14.

XXI. On Self and Others

1. For a helpful introduction to virtue ethics, see the essays gathered in Stephen Darwall, ed., *Virtue Ethics* (Blackwell, 2002). Several scholars (myself included) have argued that Smith himself deserves to be seen as a virtue ethicist; see, e.g., Deirdre McCloskey, "Adam Smith, the Last of the Former Virtue Ethicists," *History of Political Economy* 40 (2008).
2. *Theory of Moral Sentiments*, 32.
3. *Theory of Moral Sentiments*, 30.
4. *Theory of Moral Sentiments*, 175.
5. *Theory of Moral Sentiments*, 30.

XXII. On Perfection

1. I think the concept of perfection is central to Smith. Others read him as less invested in the idea of perfection; see, e.g., Forman-Barzilai, *Adam Smith and the Circles of Sympathy*.
2. *Theory of Moral Sentiments*, 33; see also 291.
3. *Theory of Moral Sentiments*, 255.

XXIII. On Wisdom and Virtue

1. Smith, consistent with his times, speaks of "the wise and virtuous man." Consistent with our times, and as Smith gives us no reason not to, I have felt free to speak also of "the wise and virtuous person."
2. See, for example, Hannah Arendt, *The Human Condition*, 2nd ed. (Chicago, 1998), esp. 7–17 and 289–94.
3. *Theory of Moral Sentiments*, 291–92.

XXIV. On Humility and Beneficence

1. Plato, *Republic*, 516c–e.
2. *Theory of Moral Sentiments*, 291–92.
3. *Theory of Moral Sentiments*, 292.
4. *Theory of Moral Sentiments*, 277.
5. *Theory of Moral Sentiments*, 269.

XXV. On Praise and Praiseworthiness

1. *Theory of Moral Sentiments*, 152.
2. *Theory of Moral Sentiments*, 284.
3. *Theory of Moral Sentiments*, 291–292.
4. *Theory of Moral Sentiments*, 135.
5. *Theory of Moral Sentiments*, 170.
6. *Theory of Moral Sentiments*, 365.

XXVI. On Socrates

1. Benjamin Franklin, *Autobiography*, in *Franklin: Writings*, ed. J. A. Leo Lemay (Library of America, 1987), 1383–85.
2. See Nehamas, *Art of Living*, and especially its treatments of Montaigne and Nietzsche and Foucault in its second part.
3. *Theory of Moral Sentiments*, 17–18.
4. *Theory of Moral Sentiments*, 282.
5. *Theory of Moral Sentiments*, 60.
6. *Theory of Moral Sentiments*, 281.
7. *Theory of Moral Sentiments*, 335.
8. *Theory of Moral Sentiments*, 295.
9. See, for example, Plato, *Apology*, 31c–e.
10. *Theory of Moral Sentiments*, 344.

XXVII. On Jesus

1. *Theory of Moral Sentiments*, 31, 198, 353–54.
2. Among many other studies, see David Sorkin, *The Religious Enlightenment* (Princeton, 2008).

3. Hume, *Natural History of Religion*, esp. sections 3 and 13.
4. *Theory of Moral Sentiments*, 197.
5. *Theory of Moral Sentiments*, 154.
6. *Theory of Moral Sentiments*, 195.
7. See, e.g., Leo Strauss, "Jerusalem and Athens: Some Preliminary Reflections," in *Studies in Platonic Political Philosophy*, ed. Thomas Pangle (Chicago, 1983).

XXVIII. On Hume

1. *Correspondence of Adam Smith*, letter 208, 251.
2. Plato, *Phaedo*, 118a.
3. *Correspondence of Adam Smith*, letter 178, 218–19.
4. *Correspondence of Adam Smith*, letter 178, 220.
5. *Correspondence of Adam Smith*, letter 178, 221.
6. Dennis Rasmussen, *The Infidel and the Professor: David Hume, Adam Smith, and the Friendship That Shaped Modern Thought* (Princeton, 2017), 222.
7. Not all scholars agree. In addition to Rasmussen's book cited just above, see, e.g., Gavin Kennedy, "Adam Smith on Religion," in *Oxford Handbook of Adam Smith*, ed. Christopher J. Berry, Maria Pia Paganelli, and Craig Smith (Oxford, 2013).

XXIX. On God

1. See also *Theory of Moral Sentiments*, 297.
2. *Theory of Moral Sentiments*, 278–79.
3. *Theory of Moral Sentiments*, 144–45.
4. *Theory of Moral Sentiments*, 278 and 45.
5. *Theory of Moral Sentiments*, 344; see also 326–27.
6. For the poles of this debate, compare D. D. Raphael and A. L. Macfie's introduction to the Glasgow edition of *The Theory of Moral Sentiments*, which emphasizes what Smith shares with Stoicism, to Eric Schliesser, *Adam Smith: Systematic Philosopher and Public Thinker* (Oxford, 2018), which distances him from it.
7. *Theory of Moral Sentiments*, 191.

Epilogue. Why Smith Now?

1. Charles Taylor, *A Secular Age* (Harvard, 2007).
2. See, e.g., Bruno Frey and Alois Stutzer, *Happiness and Economics* (Princeton, 2002).
3. An outline of UN SDG1 (and the secretary-general's annual statements of progress toward it) can be found at https://sustainabledevelopment.un.org/sdg1.

4. *Wealth of Nations*, 1:115.
5. See Hadot, *Philosophy as a Way of Life*, 264–76; Nehamas, *Art of Living*, 1–5.
6. *Theory of Moral Sentiments*, 370–71.
7. *Theory of Moral Sentiments*, 315.
8. *Theory of Moral Sentiments*, 387.
9. *Wealth of Nations*, 2:273–74.

Acknowledgments

———— ✶ ————

I am incredibly fortunate—blessed is the word that keeps coming to mind—to be a scholar of Adam Smith. Spending years with Smith himself has been a joy. But it has been no less a joy to be able to spend time with a wonderful group of colleagues and friends and students who continue to teach me so much both about Smith and about life. Several friends generously read and commented on earlier drafts of material included here; I am especially grateful to Doug Den Uyl, Sam Fleischacker, Gordon Graham, and Charles Griswold for many helpful suggestions. Two dear friends outside the academy, David Applebaum and Adam Hellegers, also subjected themselves to reading the manuscript and did much to improve it (next round's on me!). An author-meets-critics session hosted by the International Adam Smith Society at its annual meeting also provided helpful feedback; I am very grateful to Keith Hankins for organizing the session, and to Karen Valihora and Brennan McDavid for their comments. And this book would simply not have come to be were it not for several people at Princeton University Press. I am especially grateful to Al Bertrand for encouraging me to take up the challenge to write it in the first place, and to Rob Tempio for seeing it through to press and for recruiting two very insightful reviewers whose comments did much to improve the final product.

This book is dedicated to my beloved daughter. Dearest Paige, I can only hope Smith has served me well in helping you discover the gift and the mystery of your own wonderful life.